EXIT WELL

EXIT WELL

UNLOCKING YOUR COMPANY'S ENTERPRISE VALUE

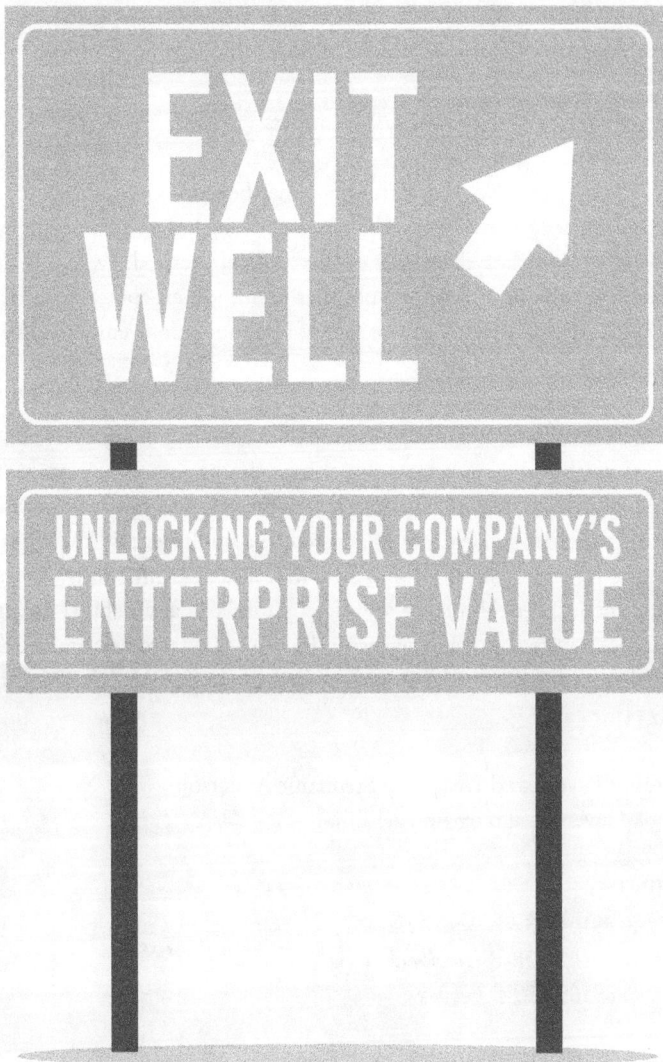

David A. Nemmers

EXIT WELL
Unlocking Your Company's Enterprise Value

Copyright © 2024 by David A. Nemmers

Interior Layout and Design by Stephanie Anderson
Book Cover Design by Abigael Elliott

ISBN:
979-8-89165-137-1 *Paperback*
979-8-89165-138-8 *Hardback*
979-8-89165-139-5 *E-book*

Published by:
Streamline Books
Kansas City, MO
streamlinebookspublishing.com

STREAMLINE BOOKS

CONTENTS

INTRODUCTION

DID IT! WHAT DID I DO? After twelve years of owning my business, I sold it. I exited, but was that really the end of the story or just the beginning?

The interesting thing about the entire process was what happened after I sold the business. I did receive the typical phone calls and emails from financial planners and wealth managers. It was amazing how fast information moved around the internet, and how illiquid and poor I was at one moment, and so popular the next. I received many phone calls and reach-outs from all sorts of people, especially other business owners, asking me how I monetized my business. The comments from the banking community were even more stunning. They offered me congratulations and told me I had done something truly difficult.

I had never given much thought to the difficulty of exiting my business, but each move I had made over those twelve years was intentional and had a specific purpose. Very simply, I did what I thought I needed to do.

One evening about two weeks after the sale and amid the transition to the new owners, I could not sleep because of all these thoughts going through my head about the deal. I crawled out of bed at 2 a.m., went downstairs, and sketched out this book, including a theme for each chapter and major bullet points.

Everyone wants to write a book, and there are plenty of good ones out there. Trust me, I have bought my fair share. Whether my book is only the result of a therapeutic process for me or it becomes a bestseller or something in between, my goal is to help other business owners maximize the value of their businesses. As I told a close friend, if writing this book helps only one small business owner prepare their business for a sale and it is successful, then all the writing, editing, more editing, re-writing, and fearing I would never finish was worth it.

If you are looking for one of those books authored by a Harvard MBA or Wharton School graduate, then keep looking. This is not one of those books. While my educational pedigree falls short of an Ivy League school or prestigious business school, my degree comes from my experience in life. According to the elites of the world, I am just a guy in flyover country, neither from the East or West Coast, but a normal Midwestern guy who grew his business and sold it twelve years later.

In my forty years of business, I have noticed several characteristics about small business owners. Keep in mind, most of the jobs in this country are created by small business owners. While the big boys or girls get all the notice (and criticisms), the backbone of our economy is the small business owner.

In my experience working with small business owners, these individuals are good, solid people who want to take care of their employees first, even to their own detriment. Funny how the media never highlights this side of capitalism, but these people exist and in much greater numbers than we even realize. There are exceptions to everything, but they are few and far between. This country is filled with hard-working men and women who take risks every day while running their own businesses.

Ultimately, those business owners face a question: How do I exit? This book will share my story and the process. Each business owner has several choices to make regarding how they wish to run and eventually exit their businesses. My way is not the only way but simply one way.

The best approach to this book is two-fold. First, read the book in its entirety before you do anything. It is important to have the endgame in mind before you start. I wrote this book in a linear fashion for a purpose. If you execute the ideas from the latter chapters first before you execute the initial chapters, you will be frustrated and spinning your wheels. If you implement the ideas in the initial chapters first, you will pave the way for the ideas in the latter chapters. If you do all this well, you will experience explosive growth and ultimately have a company worth selling at a really good price.

The chapters for this book are intentionally short. As a business owner, I despised people wasting my time. Maybe I should have had more patience, but time is one thing of which you cannot make more. The best books I read have been the ones with short, concise chapters that gave me natural stopping and starting points and, of course, had great and practical content. This book is not one of those long, heavy books written by an economics or financial professor that are rarely opened. This is a book for the small business owner, the entrepreneur.

Before I published this book, I field-tested these concepts with some actual business owners. It was one thing to take my own business through this process. The question remained, though, could I replicate the process with other businesses? In the past several years, I've taken several businesses through this process to see if it really does work. Each organization I worked with experienced a change in the way it conducted its business, and the ensuing results were outstanding. The concepts in this book are not only battled-tested within my company, but also field-tested with other companies.

This is a book for the small business owner, the entrepreneur.

I wish to thank my entire family for their support not only in the process of writing this book, but over the last twelve years of owning my business. So many people do not realize the stress and struggles small business owners face on an everyday basis. I believe the truly successful ones have an outstanding support system. My wife of forty years, Susan, has been my rock. At times I did not believe in myself, but she always believed in me, even when I was remortgaging the house and taking short-term loans from our retirement accounts, all while working long hours. Very simply, I could not have done it without her.

I also want to thank our children: Rachel; Michelle; my two sons-in-law, Eric and Patrick; Andie; Alex; and Casey (the last three coming into our family under some tragic circumstances, but that is for another book at another time). I will always be thankful for your support, kind words, and prayers over the years.

I was also blessed with an enormous friendship base. Steve, Greg, Brad, David, Mike, Linda, Ken, Chris, John, and Bob were always available for a phone call for some insights or to listen (undoubtedly, I missed someone, so please forgive me). Thank you for picking up the phone.

I hope you enjoy this book and find nuggets that can help you with your next move. One of my favorite sayings is "You can't move a parked car," so let's get moving!

CHAPTER 1

SOBERING STATISTICS

I WAS RUNNING LATE to an important meeting with my attorney. Our office was in one of the city's suburbs, about twenty minutes from my attorney's downtown office. I did not know what traffic was going to be like. Sometimes it was a breeze; other times it took over an hour. I walked into our warehouse and asked in a frantic voice, "Does anyone know where we have a hacksaw?" There I was in one of my best suits and a nice tie, looking for a hacksaw. One of my teammates, Bob, looked at me in bewilderment but said he would go grab one.

Why did I need a hacksaw? Because my old red truck, which I affectionately called Clifford after the beloved children's book character, had a hunk of rust hanging from the driver's side floorboard, almost touching the ground. Bob handed me the hacksaw and off to the parking lot I went to solve my problem, at least temporarily. I gently got down on my knees and sawed the hunk of rust away. It was about as long as my arm. I threw it into the backseat of my truck and off I went to see my attorney.

Clifford was a legend at the office, and I got many inquiries as to why I would drive such a vehicle. After all, it wasn't worth much. But to me, the old red truck was priceless. First, it was paid for, and despite the repairs and the frequent hacksaw adjustments, the truck did get me to where I needed to go. Plus, the savings from not owning a newer vehicle let me invest more into the business in the areas where we needed it the most.

Fun question: How much is a used car worth? A used car is usually worth more to the owner than to the buyer. Why is that the case? Why is there almost always some sort of discrepancy between what the used car owner thinks it is worth and what the prospective buyer thinks it is? As an owner of several used cars and trucks (the last one I traded in was my fourteen-year-old Chevy Silverado with over 355,000 miles), I can tell you the answer is simple: emotion.

Emotion gets in the way of common sense and objectivity, and I see it every day with small business owners. As they look at their businesses, they try to quantify all the risk and effort they have put into the business, and they put an enormous number on what they think their business is worth. They have built a successful business, made a living, and now they know—they just know—that they are going to sell for a lot of money and be done. It is just supposed to be that way. Work hard, build the business, and sell for big bucks. Your business, just like my old truck Clifford, is probably worth a whole lot less than you think.

Small business owners try to quantify all the risk and effort they have put into the business, and they put an enormous number on what they think their business is worth.

If you own a business, you are on an entrepreneurial journey. At some point in the future (and it is closer than you think), Father Time will catch you, and you will need to decide what you will do with your business. How will you maximize the value of your business? How will you transfer your legacy knowledge of the business to the next generation of owner?

There are hundreds of books written on the actual process of exiting your business and selling it, but there are far fewer books on how you even get to the point of selling your business. This book is the prelude to you selling the business, and what you do in advance of the sale may be the most important thing you do as you prepare to exit someday.

For many entrepreneurs, creating a business is like raising a child. They give birth to the idea; pour blood, sweat, and tears into the business; and take huge financial risks. Of course someone will pay them top dollar for their business, they believe. The sad truth is, the prospective buyer does not care about those facts. The buyer does not care how much equity, whether time or money, you have put into the business or how much risk you have taken. The buyer cares about compounded growth rates, gross margin percentages, customer acquisition costs, and EBITDA (earnings before interest, taxes, depreciation, and amortization), among other things. If you want to maximize the value of your business, you need to get over it and get on with it. This book should help you get on with it, and the "it" is placing your business in the best possible position to be sold and at a strong enterprise value.

What are the stats when it comes to selling a small business? They are not pretty. In a *Forbes* magazine article titled "Study Shows Why Many Businesses Owners Can't Sell When They Want To" written by Mary Allen Biery and Sageworks Stats, Christopher Snider, president and CEO of the Exit Planning Institute (EPI), lists some sobering statistics. In my research, these stats are consistent with other surveys, and they are eye-opening.[1] Which leads to some tough questions:

▶ As a business owner, have you thought about your transition plan? This is even more important the older you are. Mr. Snider indicates that 66 percent of businesses have no plan at all in terms of transitioning from the current owner.

▶ Have you enlisted anyone from outside your company to help with a transition? The survey shows 80 percent have not sought any help.

▶ Do you have an estimate as to the value of your business and what you will need for your financial needs in the future? The survey results show that many businesses do not know these basic facts.

▶ Is your management or leadership team ready to take over after a transition? Have you transferred the legacy knowledge to your team? The survey indicated only 25 percent of business owners were confident in their current management team.

Those stats are sobering. But here is the good news: You are not alone. Most small business owners have not given their exit much thought let alone how to maximize their business value. In fact, I loved Snider's comment that small business owners need to figure out how to "harvest" the wealth of the business. Snider points out that over the course of the next decade, more than 4.5 million firms will need to be transitioned to new owners with an estimated value of $10 trillion (yes, that is trillion with a T).

Another daunting fact is that so many small business owners have a vast amount of their personal net worth wrapped up in their businesses. Over 40 percent of small business owners have almost all of their net worth in their business. In my case, over 95 percent of my net worth was in my business, making me highly vulnerable to a potentially bad financial ending. If a sizable percentage of your net worth is in your business, you are financially very vulnerable too. You need to do something proactive to maximize the value of your organization and start reducing your financial risk. Remember the old saying that hope is not a strategy.

I really like the harvest analogy Snider used because farmers know when to harvest their crops. If they harvest too early, they leave much of the crop immature and not very sellable. If they harvest too late, much of the crop may have died, which means it's also not very sellable. Farmers understand the timing of the When and the How to maximize their crop, which means more money.

How do you harvest the wealth in your business? How do you join the minority of small business owners who have a plan and purpose in maximizing their exit?

The answer is simple but difficult to do. According to an article written for *Score* by Todd Michael Cohan titled "The Current Rise in Small Businesses Being Sold Over the Next 10-15 Years," only 20 to 30 percent of small businesses that are listed to sell actually sell each year.[2] In fact, this statistic is one of the most optimistic ones. According to Worldwide Business Brokers, only one out of 5.5 businesses get sold each year, a rate of less than 20 percent. Could you imagine in the housing market if only 20 to 30 percent of houses that were listed actually sold each year? That would be a crisis, yet no one is highlighting the crisis of selling small businesses with these sobering stats.

There is a great line in the movie *Apollo 13* after the astronauts become aware of their potential peril. Tom Hanks, playing Commander Lovell, says, "Houston, we have a problem." Yes, we have a problem transferring the tremendous wealth created by day-to-day entrepreneurs, and I am not sure anyone is listening.

I have your attention now. You are all-in. What is the answer? Remember the answer is simple but hard to do. The answer is in the form of a question: Have you created a successful *company*?

To exit well and maximize your business, you first must create a successful company, not just a business. This sometimes can take years to do. This is not an overnight project, and I am sorry I do not have a magic pill. You must have a plan, you must execute with purpose, and you must be hyper-focused.

At this point, I am guessing I have scared about 20 percent of the readers away. They are running back to the store or online for a refund on this book. Believe it or not, if you are in that 20 percent, it is okay to get a refund and put the book away, just don't be too disappointed with the price you will receive for your business when you do exit (if you can exit at all). Another 20 percent

To exit well and maximize your business, you first must create a successful company, not just a business.

7

of you are completely sold and want to execute today and sell tomorrow. Although I appreciate your enthusiasm, this process takes time. In a society that demands results yesterday, my approach is not a popular one, but I am not going to set unrealistic expectations. Please do not let your enthusiasm turn into frustration when you do not see the results right away. If done well, you will not be disappointed.

For the remaining 60 percent of you, I have your attention, but I do not want to become another business book you read and check off your list. I have personally owned hundreds of those books, some of which I never read (I guess I thought I would get smarter through osmosis). My goal is that this book will help you set your direction, and with every decision you make, you will have the end in mind.

Do not become a sobering statistic and look back someday on your business and wonder, *What if I had done something differently?*

I challenge you to become hyper-focused and build a great company. The results will be worth it.

NEXT STEPS

▶ Do you know how much money you need to retire to maintain your current lifestyle? Warning: The number is bigger than you think.

▶ Do you know how much your business is worth? Note: Even a back-of-the-napkin approach from an experienced CPA or a merger and acquisition firm is helpful, but remember that the market ultimately determines how much your business is worth.

▶ How big of a gap is there between how much money you need to retire and the value of your business (and other non-business assets)? How do you close the gap? How many years do you have before you retire?

CHAPTER 2

WHY?

PEERED INTO THE HOUSE from the backyard and saw a scene playing out in the kitchen that I had seen too often as a kid. My dad was sitting just inside the window at a small table with two chairs tucked in the corner.

On most nights, my dad would come home exhausted from his journeyman electrician job. It was a bone-tired exhaustion. His typical routine after he put his car into the undersized garage was to take the short walk to the house and sit in a chair in the kitchen. My mom had his favorite drink waiting for him. He cherished his whisky and water. Most nights, it was just one drink, then he would clean up for dinner, then have a little downtime, then go to bed, and then go to battle again the next day. But on those nights when he needed to have two drinks, I knew the news was not going to be good. Two drinks, especially on a Friday evening, meant he had been laid off.

The actual event of the layoff was never the issue; it was part of being in the construction industry. The issue was the aftermath of the layoff. It was the belt tightening, the spending as little as possible until a new job became available. To this day, my dislike for spaghetti stems from these periods of time. The only way mom could make ends meet for a family of seven was to feed us spaghetti on a regular basis.

By all accounts, we were a blue collar family. We lived paycheck to paycheck, but we always had enough food and clothing (though not a lot of either one) and a roof over our heads. Life was never easy, and as I reflect on my mom, who passed away at age ninety-six, she was the best CEO I ever knew. Maybe it was because she grew up in the Great Depression, and by comparison to her upbringing, she may have felt rich even in our strapped circumstances. She found a way to make it work even with the most meager of incomes.

My outlook on life and work was shaped by my dad being laid-off and the on-again, off-again work of the construction industry. My father had a ninth-grade education. He was from the Greatest Generation (born in the 1920s, served in World War II, etc.). While not a highly educated man by today's standards, he was very bright, and his mechanical skills were exceptional. He could fix almost anything. I do think those skills skip generations. I am not nearly as mechanically inclined as he was.

My dad's working career comprised a variety of jobs through the union on various job sites, including working the Alaskan pipeline in the 1970s. As with many people in the construction industry, the sector varies with the economy, and he was laid off dozens of times during his career. While the layoffs had a negative impact on the family, the one item of note that stayed with me the most was the lack of personal connectivity my father had with each of his employers. They never or rarely ever knew his name.

For some reason, the "never knew your name" syndrome stuck with me, and I pledged to myself no matter what role I had in an organization, I would know the names of everyone, from the highest to the lowest position in the company, plus the names of their spouses and children (and in many cases, grandchildren).

My goal, or better yet, my Why, of owning a business was deeply rooted in this childhood experience. I never wanted a teammate of mine to feel like a cog in the wheel. Employees, which I prefer to call teammates, elect to spend forty-plus hours a week at their workplace. This is a significant portion of their week and ultimately their lives.

If there is no connectivity across the organization, something in each person dies a little each day. I wanted to be different. I wanted to do something that created value for all stakeholders. Trust me, I had my doubters, and their criticism still rings in my mind. They argued a goal like mine was not attainable. But my dad's story helped me persevere and create a company which I would say to this day was and still is special. We understood our Why.

Why did you decide to start or buy an existing business? Before you can even think about your exit, you must first have an honest conversation with yourself as to why you decided to own a business.

Simon Sinek wrote a great book called *Start with Why*. Sinek's major theme is that an organization needs to define it's Why. Many organizations get a little confused about this. Sinek points out it is not what you do or even how you do it, but why you do it.[3]

What is so important about understanding your business's Why? Because your team needs to be on the same page as you, especially your leadership team. If your team has different Why's than you, I can guarantee you will have major issues along the way when it comes to strategy, planning, and execution of that strategy. While healthy conflict is a sign of a vibrant organization, I have seen so many times when shareholders, leaders, and the team have different Whys, which leads to challenges and, in some cases, corporate chaos.

But before you decide on the organization's Why, I believe you need to start at the very beginning and define why you do the whole business thing in the first place.

> Before you can even think about your exit, you must first have an honest conversation with yourself as to why you decided to own a business.

My personal Why of owning a business and the Why of the company are somewhat intertwined and have strong roots in my upbringing.

When you get a chance to own a business, you need to understand why you're doing it. Everyone is different, and each Why of a company by and large is not better or worse than the other. If your only goal is to make a lot of money, I believe you will be disappointed, if not now, then in the future. The entrepreneurs I know put in long hours; are typically the last ones to get paid, especially in a downturn; and find ways to help their employees even at the expense of their own pockets.

You may be thinking this sounds really "millennial like"—profits don't matter, only people. Let me put up a huge caution flag. I have been accused (and insulted) on this profit-versus-people discussion from both sides. I once had an employee who, while we were having lunch that I paid for, told me he was very disappointed in me because I put profit before people. At the same time, one of the private equity firms that was a minority partner chastised me for putting people before profits. Because I was getting beat up by both sides, I probably got it just right.

For you to do good things with your business, resources, and people, you must first make money. But making money allows you to invest in your people, which in turn allows you to make more money. Making money is not a dirty word, as some would suggest. I laugh that many think capitalism is a great evil that has created all the problems of the world. Milton Friedman, an American economist who received the 1976 Nobel Memorial Prize in Economic Sciences on capitalism, famously said this in a 1979 interview with Phil Donahue:

> "In the only cases in which the masses have escaped from the kind of grinding poverty you're talking about, the only cases in recorded history, are where they have had capitalism and largely free trade. If you want to know where the masses are worse off, it's exactly in the kinds of societies that depart from that. So that the record of history is absolutely crystal clear, that there is no alternative way so far discovered of improving the lot of the ordinary people that can hold a candle to the productive activities that are unleashed by the free-enterprise system."[4]

In my simple way of looking at things, making money matters. You must make money first, but the true test is what you do with it. The U.S. Bureau of Labor Statistics (BLS) has some sobering facts related to new businesses. According to Investopedia, "Data from the BLS shows that approximately 20% of new businesses fail during the first two years of being open, 45% during the first five years, and 65% during the first 10 years. Only 25% of new businesses make it to 15 years or more."[5] For wannabe entrepreneurs, the chances of still being in business in ten years are one in three. Yet despite the odds, risks, and high levels of stress, according to statistics by the Commerce Institute, a record 5.5 million businesses were started last year.[6] This would be an average of over 15,000 new businesses each and every day of the year. Entrepreneurship is still alive and well.

> You must make money first, but the true test is what you do with it.

What does this have to do with your Why and eventually exiting your business? Everything. Understanding your Why is the foundation of your exit.

If your Why for your business is simply a lifestyle company or a micro-job, understand this approach can and probably will work year in and year out, but you will probably not maximize the value of your business. If your goal is a comfortable living with limited hours (you own the business, you get to make the choices) and/or you aim to run as many family expenses through the business, you will not maximize the value of your company. Side note: Running personal expenses through your business is against IRS rules, but I see it day in and day out.

If your desire is to leave the business to your kids, keep in mind that only about 30 percent of businesses make it to the second generation, if they make it through the first ten years. I decided early on I would not have my children or any family members in the business. First of all, I think it is a disservice to the family member. The only reason they got the job was because they are related to the owner. More importantly, it may not be in the best interest of the company. I have watched a first-generation owner sell his business with his children still involved, and it was downright messy. Does the owner make the decision that is best for him or best for his kids? Where is the conflict, and how does it get resolved? Are there lasting effects of the decision? Again, if your decision is to have your kids in the business, it is a choice that will ultimately impact your exit and the value received. And I won't debate your children's skills and talent levels; we all believe our kids are the best.

I would challenge you as you read this book to understand the impact of your Why on your possible exit. If you are okay with a lower value for your business because you run it as a lifestyle company or your children are involved, that is fine, but be honest with yourself.

As I indicated earlier, my personal Why was influenced by my father's working experience and my faith. I believe I am simply a steward of the organization. As I defined the company's Why, I needed to make sure my leadership team was on the same page (more on leadership in the next chapter). As my leadership team and I worked through the process of understanding the company's Why, we found out we were all on the same page.

Our Why was simple: We value people. This included our customers, teammates, vendors, and all stakeholders in the company. Because my leadership team and I had agreement, all our decisions were rooted in that simple statement, "We value people." Valuing people didn't mean we didn't value profit, but those two P's work hand in hand with each other. You can't do one without the other. If done right, you can create an organization where people want to come to work and enjoy success both professionally and financially (more on the financial side later).

Understanding the Why helps you understand what you do and how you do it. For me, it brought great clarity not only for me, but for my entire team as well.

So, what is your Why?

NEXT STEPS

► Define why you decided to start or buy a business in the first place.

► What is your company's Why? Below are a couple of examples:
  ▼ Apple: "With everything we do, we aim to challenge the status quo."
  ▼ Southwest Airlines: "We are the champion of the common man."
    ► Note: In both examples, they didn't highlight products or services. Instead, they focused on why they were in business. Notice they didn't say profit.

► Does your leadership team (and eventually your entire corporate team) know, believe, and live out the company's Why? If not, how do you message your Why to your team?

CHAPTER 3

THE FOUNDATION

LOOKED AROUND AT MY AUDIENCE and asked, "Would you hire yourself?" The silence was deafening, so I asked again, "Would you hire yourself?" Again, nothing but silence.

I get the opportunity to speak in front of groups from time to time. Audiences range from a classroom of high school students to hundreds of business owners. That night, I had an opportunity to speak to a class of college students. One of the students had asked me to speak to his class about owning a business. The class was a study in entrepreneurship, made up of about thirty students. The room we met in was perfect for my talk. It was not a large auditorium with stadium-style seating, but a small room where I could stand up and engage the students in a much more personal manner.

My approach to dealing with nerves when it comes to public speaking has evolved over time, and one of the calming techniques I have found that works well for me is to walk around while I talk. In a larger venue, this is a little more challenging, but on that night, the room was perfect. By walking around, I created a more casual environment, which kept my audience engaged.

My talks take the audience through my entrepreneurial journey. My typical starting point for most of my talks is to ask the audience what they want to get out of our time together. This little trick allowed me to accomplish a couple of things. First, it allowed me to get the audience engaged right from the start. This approach allows the audience to feel part of the discussion from the beginning and allows for a more robust discussion. Second, it allowed me to change my presentation to meet the needs and expectations of my listeners.

When I opened with that question to the college students, one theme became clear from their answers. They wanted to know if they could really do it. Could they start or buy a business and be their own boss?

When most people hear someone is a business owner, they assume all the wrong things. Most people think being a business owner means you are on Easy Street. You can come and go as you please, you are not accountable to anyone for anything, you have unlimited vacation time, and of course you make all kinds of money.

The assumption is once you own a business, you have made it, and it is time to start ordering fancy cars and buy a big house. This assumption is far from reality and is, quite frankly, the exact opposite of reality.

The assumption that being a business owner means you are on Easy Street is far from reality.

I tried to bring a little reality to the students that night, because many of those assumptions were firmly ingrained in their minds. I took them through my journey of owning a business. I had attempted to start several over my career, ranging from a franchise to my own consulting firm, with some elements of success and lots of failures along the way.

My last venture into owning a business was my biggest bet. At the age of forty-six, I borrowed millions of dollars to buy a business in an industry I knew nothing about. When I look back, I ask myself what I was thinking. If I had been advising myself on whether to buy a business with no experience in the industry, I would have recommended passing on the opportunity.

I shared with my audience how I tripled the size of the business, increased profitability, and was honored to have my business named as one of the best places to work in the area several years in a row. I also shared the stress of hitting bank covenants, making sure I had enough money for payroll, and funding the business for growth.

I recounted the valleys of remortgaging the house at least three times, rolling my retirement accounts into the business, and one of the humblest experiences, asking my wife to roll her retirement accounts into the business as well.

I told them about the times we sat on the verge of insolvency or at least it felt like we were going in that direction. You take all that stress, and then you add in the naysayers (both internally and externally) who will tell you only the things you are doing wrong. They essentially call you incompetent. It is at those times when you must dig deep, believe in yourself and your team, and persevere.

I could tell by the students' eyes and body language they were riveted by the story. It busted their paradigms of owning their own businesses and probably scared a few away. I had one more mic-drop moment for them. Before I opened up for questions, I asked them to list the attributes of teammates they would hire if they owned a business while keeping in mind that they had leveraged all their assets and could lose everything if the business failed.

The list we produced that night was outstanding. They listed attributes such as honesty, integrity, hard work, showing up on time, communicating effectively, being a team player, and servant-style leadership, just to name a few. Then I asked them, "Would you hire yourself?" Silence. I asked again. Silence. I let the silence linger in the room.

I then asked a second question to break the stalemate: "Who would you hire in this room?" It was a little awkward, but finally a student raised his hand. I could see a pained expression on his face. He said, "I don't know if I would hire myself or anyone else in my class." As I concluded our talk, which had become more of a discussion, I stressed that the greatest thing you can do for your business is selecting the right leaders for your team.

Years ago, when I had bet everything I owned on buying a particular company, my leadership team comprised of five individuals who had been in the industry for decades. At our first leadership meeting after I took the helm, I could tell their confidence level was apprehensive at best. The best part of the leadership team was their experience, but that was also a drawback. While they knew the industry extremely well, the business had plateaued for several years. The business was not growing, and I believed it would eventually die if we did not move in a different direction.

I know it sounds cliché, but all solidly built houses or buildings have one thing in common: a firm foundation. If you do not have a firm foundation, it does not matter how amazing the structure is that you put on top because it will not last.

In the Bible, there is a remarkable story of a wise builder and a foolish builder. It is found in Matthew 7:24-27, which reads:

> Therefore everyone who hears these words of mine
> and puts them into practice is like a wise man who

built his house on the rock. The rain came down, the streams rose, and the winds blew and beat against that house; yet it did not fall, because it had its foundation on the rock. But everyone who hears these words of mine and does not put them into practice is like a foolish man who built his house on sand. The rain came down, the streams rose, and the winds blew and beat against that house, and it fell with a great crash.

Whether you are a student of the Bible, a casual reader of it, or have never read it, the idea is clear. It all starts with the foundation. Tough times or storms will come to your business. I guarantee it. Besides death and taxes, it is certain you will have some challenging times. A business built on a solid foundation will not get swept away and crash. How firm is your business foundation?

What does a solid foundation have to do with monetizing your business? As with a house or building, a firm foundation is the key. Without it, everything will crumble. If you do not build a solid foundation in your business, you will not maximize your enterprise value.

Some people get lucky in that they develop an amazing product and, boom, someone comes in and gives them an incredible deal. This diving catch, as I call it, does happen, but more than likely you need to build your business to sell it, step by step, and it starts with a single foundational item. If you do this well, all the other steps in this book build upon it, and the success and speed increase exponentially if you have a solid foundation. But if you do not have a solid foundation, nothing you build will last. It may last for a period, with moments of teetering, but once those business storms come, everything will collapse. A business that can survive the storms is a business worth owning—and eventually selling.

> **If you do not build a solid foundation in your business, you will not maximize your enterprise value.**

What is this magic foundation, and where can you purchase it? Some of you may be hoping you can get it from Amazon Prime the next day. Unfortunately, this may be the most difficult piece of monetizing your business. If done well, it will more than likely set you up for success and an exit at a great price. If done poorly, frustration awaits around the corner. Why do it? Everything hinges on it if you want to exit well.

The foundational item is leadership and your leadership team. John C. Maxwell wrote one of the best leadership books around, *The 21 Irrefutable Laws of Leadership*.[7] If you have not read it, I highly recommend it (and no, I do not receive any monetary compensation for suggested books). To me, Maxwell's first law is the most important. The other laws are important too, but the first one is key. Maxwell's first irrefutable law is the Law of the Lid. He explains it like this:

> "Leadership ability is always the lid on person-al and organizational effectiveness. If a person's leadership ability is high, then the organization's lid is high. But if it's not, then the organization is limited."

Put another way, it is all about leadership. Maxwell would say "everything rises and falls based on leadership."

You may grasp the concept that you need good leaders, but it starts with you first. You must look at yourself and ask an important question: Are you the lid on the organization? This can really hurt if you are honest with yourself. If you are the lid, your company will never reach its full potential, and you will never exit well.

Most entrepreneurs cannot successfully navigate this issue of leadership without some help. They may have delusions of grandeur, thinking they are infallible because, after all, they built the business. Or, their egos are so large they are blinded by reality. If you really want to know if you are the lid, you need to do some work.

First, you need to get some input from your team about your leadership skills as well as about your strengths and weaknesses. Make sure you give them grace to be honest with you. The best way to do this is have someone take the lead in collecting feedback in a confidential manner and assimilate all the information for your review. Second, you need to either be accountable to an outside board or advisory board and get their honest feedback. Then, based on this feedback, get to work.

Other options include bringing in an outside strategic coach. Along with being accountable to an outside board, I hired a strategic coach, and it was like getting a quarterly colonoscopy—without sedation. It was not pleasant, but it made me think differently, made me better, and eventually made the company better. An entire book can be written on hiring a strategic coach, but my suggestion is to find one with a proven track record. Interview several and choose the one with whom you have the best connection but who is not a "yes" person.

The other option is leveraging private equity firms. On separate occasions over the twelve years I owned my business, I had two private equity firms own minority positions. These minority owners created a greater discipline for me, even though they did not have voting control, and increased my level of accountability. Both options may give you feedback you may not enjoy (and trust me, at times, I did not enjoy it), but it will make you better. It will raise your leadership lid.

One of the items of input from my team on my leadership skills was that I was terrible at hiring new people for the organization. They told me I simply liked everyone. While it was sobering feedback because I felt I could discern good people from bad, the data told me something else. My success rate with new hires was only about 25 percent.

As I look back on my hiring decisions over my tenure at the company, I wasted millions (yes, millions) of dollars on bad hires. What did I do with this feedback? I took the feedback to heart and let the team produce a hiring process that allowed me to have input only after several vetting interviews had taken place without me. In some cases, they did not even need me (or want me) to do any type of interview. Guess what happened?

Our success rate rose to almost 90 percent on new hires, and the team felt empowered to make hiring decisions and were fully vested and accountable to the new team members' success. I was the lid on the hiring process and success. By getting out of the way and playing to my team members' strengths, we made the entire company better.

Once you address your personal leadership skills and limitations, you need to address your leadership team. Your business will only be as good as this group of people according to the Law of the Lid. I have seen so many scenarios where there is an issue in a particular department of an organization or discipline, and most of the problem, and sometimes the sole source of the problem, is the leader of that area. I have seen on many occasions where a department or group is failing or not achieving the desired results not through the fault of the group, but because of poor leadership.

My initial leadership team when I purchased the business was quite different than the leadership team when I sold it. I had only one person left from the original leadership team when I exited the business. All the other positions, except for one, were hired from outside the company and, believe it or not, outside the industry. The original members of the leadership team, while all good people, either took on other duties within the company or left of their own accord.

If you wish to exit well, especially if you do not want to continue with the business, you must have a fully functional leadership team that executes well. This foundational item takes time. Most business owners do not have the patience for this step, yet this is the most crucial step.

You must first hire well. You must make sure they are the right fit and, above all, they have the right character. While I went outside the industry to hire my leadership team, this is not a prerequisite. I hired based on character first; they could learn the industry. Many people in that industry—I affectionately call them industry snobs—believe you cannot be successful if you do not have specific industry experience. I will continue to disagree with those snobs and contend that the first step is to hire character first.

The second step, once you get them on board, is to invest in them,

> If you wish to exit well, you must have a fully functional leadership team that executes well.

especially if they do not know the industry. It is imperative they understand the industry from top to bottom, and the only way to do this is through time and by placing them in the right opportunities to learn. For those who want this to happen fast, they will be disappointed, because investment in your leadership team takes time. So, you better get started now.

Do you want to build a great company? Do you want to exit well? It starts with you first and then your leadership team. This is the foundation of your business and the key to your exit. Invest in yourself, and invest in your team with tools and resources that help them develop as leaders. These changes take time. Finding the right people takes time. If you hire from outside your industry, it takes time. My suggestion is to get moving, right now!

NEXT STEPS

▶ How do you rate yourself as a leader? Can you get some objective feedback on your leadership ability? Can you hire a strategic coach? Can you find an advisory board?

▶ How do you rate your current leadership team? What additional training or resources do they need? How can you invest in them? Do they know and believe in the company's Why?

▶ Which members of your leadership team need to stay and which need to go either elsewhere in the company or outside it? What new leaders do you need to hire, if any?

CHAPTER 4

COMMON LANGUAGE

YOU COULD SEE THE EXCITEMENT (or maybe it was terror) on my face as I got myself settled into my desk at the company that I had just bought. There I was at the age of forty-six fulfilling my dream of owning a business. The risks at that age were great. I was placing everything on the line, but I envisioned something special.

My new office space was a major decision for me. I desired an open-door policy for all my teammates, and a formal, stuffy office was not the best option. I decided on day one to have my office on the floor with the team in a tiny, windowless, six-by-six cubicle. The upside of the space was that I was tucked into the corner, so traffic was minimal, but the team knew I was there on the floor with them.

Our first office space was a drab gray color with office furniture that was decades old. You could smell and see years' worth of dust, grime, and wear on the cubicle walls. The carpet was so well-worn in some spots that you could see past the padding and all the way to the foundation. Regardless, this was my company, and we were going to do some great things right away—or so I believed.

The honeymoon period with a new company can be several months or even years, but I was in for a rude awakening. I had bought the business with a partner (whom I later bought out), and he was going to be the inside guy handling operations while I was going to be responsible for sales.

The first week was spent getting to know the team and allowing the team to get to know us as the new owners. That week was like the dreaded first date. A little awkward at times, but each side wants to know a little bit more about the other. We had meetings, lunch appointments with teammates, and a chance to go around and meet everyone.

The first week ended uneventfully, and I was ready to hit the ground running on the second Monday. Little did I know I was heading into communication chaos.

Since sales was my responsibility, I wanted to know on Monday morning from the sales team the answer to one simple question: What did you book in sales the previous week? In my mind, a sales booking was an order or formal commitment from a customer for our products or services.

I walked around the dated office with the dated furniture and that smell (which I can still smell today) and asked each salesperson that simple question. At first, I got some blank stares, because apparently, I was not following the process. The process in the past involved passing around a sheet of paper at the Tuesday morning meeting on which each salesperson wrote down their bookings for the previous week.

My expectations were a little different. I did not want to wait until Tuesday morning to find out what sales we had won the previous week. After all, a salesperson should know by Monday morning what they had sold the previous week. It didn't seem overly complicated to me. With some reluctance from the team at having a new process, I collected the sales booking data for the prior week. The data was helpful, and it seemed like we had a productive bookings week, so I was off to meet with customers with my new teammates.

I repeated the same process the following week, much to the chagrin of the sales team. They gave me a look as if to say, "Are you really going to ask me this question every Monday? This is very annoying." The sales team's attitude to this new process was like the old office environment we were in, stale and outdated. They did not like it.

The team humored me with the sales booking data, and to my surprise (it was more shocking than surprising), much of the data they gave me for the second week was identical to the first week. I was perplexed. Did we sell the exact same thing to the same customer two weeks in a row? I thought it was possible, but I needed to dig a little further. Once I dug into the numbers, I was in disbelief.

During my discussions with each sales team member, I found out that each had a different definition of a sales booking. Remember, my definition of a sales booking was an order (via a purchase order) or other formal commitment from a customer that they want to buy our products or services. However, the definition of a sales booking among the team members was as unique as each salesperson.

One salesperson (I will call him Mr. Optimist) booked a sale when a customer was inquiring about a project or service with us. There was no commitment, only an inquiry as to a potential solution and the cost related to that solution. I had another salesperson (I will call her Mrs. Pessimist) who would only book a sale once the project was complete and paid for by the customer. Each salesperson had their own definition of a sales booking.

We had a problem. We could not communicate at even a basic level as a team. We had a long way to go. We needed a common language.

This is the next important step after laying your strong foundation. You have looked in the mirror and assessed yourself with the help of others, and you have assessed your leadership team, making any necessary changes, because as John C. Maxwell said, "everything rises and falls on leadership." You now have good leaders, you have determined you are not the lid of the organization, and you may be thinking you are done. You can let the leaders lead, get out of the way, and watch your business go off to the races, right? Sorry, it really does not work that way. You have established the foundation, and now it is time to build on it. In my opinion, this is where the fun stuff starts to happen.

As you read this book, you will notice several biblical references. While you do not have to be a believer in the Bible, there are some outstanding management concepts and gems in it. One of my favorite Bible stories is about the Tower of Babel. The story highlights what I call the Tower of Babel syndrome that so many organizations face each day. This syndrome is a huge barrier to an organization's success and ultimately the enterprise value. The story is found in Genesis 11:1-9:

> Now the whole world had one language and a common speech. As people moved eastward, they found a plain in Shinar and settled there.
>
> They said to each other, "Come, let's make bricks and bake them thoroughly." They used brick instead of stone, and tar for mortar. Then they said, "Come, let us build ourselves a city, with a tower that reaches to the heavens, so that we may make a name for ourselves; otherwise, we will be scattered over the face of the whole earth."
>
> But the LORD came down to see the city and the tower the people were building. The LORD said, "If as one people speaking the same language, they have begun to do this, then nothing they

plan to do will be impossible for them. Come, let us go down and confuse their language so they will not understand each other."

So the LORD scattered them from there over all the earth, and they stopped building the city. That is why it was called Babel—because there the LORD confused the language of the whole world. From there the LORD scattered them over the face of the whole earth.

You may have heard this story before, but what does this have to do with business? The message is "one language and a common speech." Once you have your leadership team in place, if you do not speak the same common language, you will spend considerable time in meetings just trying to get a basic understanding of any topic. This is the Tower of Babel syndrome.

At this point, some of you may be thinking this is going to be a lesson in the language of business, such as accounting, finance, debits, credits, and the like, and you simply want to run away from such terms. While accounting and finance are critical to your business and decision making, there are some fundamental things that need to be defined before you get to the dreaded numbers.

In my company, we as a team needed to address the booking definition, but I knew that was a short-term solution. If the sales team did not have consensus on something as simple as a sales booking, I knew we had a larger problem as an organization.

What did we stand for as a business, what were the foundational items we were going to build our business upon, and did everyone know them and believe in them? Common language is a necessary element of creating culture, and I was not going to change the culture of the business if we did not have a common language. Where was I to start?

The place to start in developing your business's common language is your values. This is a key item for all your decisions. I must confess, I did not hire outside consultants or do much internal polling to determine our values. I simply put into writing those unmovable items which should be in our corporate DNA.

Your values should be simple to understand and simple to remember. We built our values around "three I's." Our values were Integrity, Innovation, and Impact. Most team-mates could remember the three I's, and we included them in their respective performance reviews. We did expand the definition of the values to the following:

If you do not speak the same common language, you will spend considerable time in meetings just trying to get a basic understanding of any topic.

▶ **INTEGRITY:**
We will conduct business in a manner that is honest, trust-worthy, respectful, and consistent with biblically based principles.

▶ **INNOVATION:**
We will deliver to our customers extraordinary performance.

▶ **IMPACT:**
We will make a positive impact on our co-workers and their families by creating a work environment that builds char-acter, strengthens individuals, and nurtures families; and on the community by giving back with both our time and financial resources.

As you look at those values, you will see a correlation into our company Why, "We value people." Your values should reflect your Why. Unfortunately, so many companies never understand their Why or their corresponding values and are subject to the dreaded curse of "business drift." Business drift occurs when a company has no vision or direction and just drifts day in and day out. Those companies eventually drift themselves out of business.

Many of our teammates could not recite the definitions of our values verbatim, but they were published. We had a large display in our lobby of our values for our customers and guests to see. Most importantly, our employees saw the leadership team live out those values each day. Living out those values is the most important element of our business. If you publish those values and do not live them each day, you erode trust within your company. If you make a decision that violates integrity (maybe a decision you make that generates more money but may be a little shady), it sets the bar for the rest of the company. Your teammates are watching.

Does it work, or is this more gobbledygook from the over-priced and overvalued consulting world? I had an employee tell me after the fact about a decision he made in which he could have generated thousands of dollars of additional profit for the company at the expense of the customer, and the customer would never have known. However, he chose to do the right thing for the customer and made the adjusted price lower, which meant our profit was a little lower. He knew the right thing to do and saw day in and day out the leadership team living out the values of the company. Yes, values work if you live them out.

Once you have your values defined, you must define your other key business terms. Let us start with the biggest business term no one wants to define: success. What does success look like? How do you know your company is successful? Are you on the same page as your leadership team and the entire employee base? If you asked a rank-and-file teammate if he could tell you if the company or even if he was successful today, could he tell you?

So many organizations fail in the area of knowing what success looks like and whether everyone is driven to the same definition of success. You need to spend time with your leadership team on defining success, get input from the entire organization, and then pound out the message every day in a variety of ways.

It is also very key for your teammates to understand success. Nothing is worse than just showing up to work for a paycheck. These types of employees are the unmotivated type, are subject to burnout, and will leave on a moment's notice for an extra dollar. To build a great company, you need great teammates, and everyone must know how to define success.

Spend time with your leadership team on defining success, get input from the entire organization, and then pound out the message every day in a variety of ways.

At the beginning of each year at my company, we would gather everyone together for our annual corporate launch meeting. At the meeting, we discussed the highs and lows of the previous year and, most importantly, our goals and objectives for the coming year. This launch was the foundation of our communication to the team. Every corporate communication went back to the annual meeting and our goals and objectives for the year.

One of the ways we highlighted success and tracked our progress against our goals and objectives in our company was a weekly email from me to the entire company called Wins for the Week. Each Monday morning when employees logged into their computers, the Wins for the Week email would be waiting for them. The email highlighted great stories from the previous week about how we as a company were successful. The win could have been a big deal that was booked or an extraordinary customer service interaction. As an example of the latter, we once had a customer who spoke only Spanish, and the customer service teammate was having a hard time helping her. The customer service teammate knew one of our technicians spoke fluent Spanish and connected the two, even though it was after hours. Not only did we solve the customer's problem, but we also made her very happy.

The Wins for the Week reflected our values through short stories, highlighting teammates who were living out those values in our business. If you read the stories over and over, it reinforced how we were going to go about doing business as well as how we were going to take care of our customers and, most importantly, each other. It takes a lot of time to change a culture, but only through common language can you do it.

What are those key definitions you need to know? What does an exceptional customer experience look like? How do you define quality? How do you define employee engagement? What is a sale (sounds fundamental, but some companies struggle even with basic definitions)? While this may seem overwhelming, do not major in the minors. Define your success and those elements that make up that definition of success, then communicate it frequently. Once done, you will eliminate any "business babel."

NEXT STEPS

▶ What are your corporate values? Are those values shared by your leadership team and the entire company?

▶ How do you communicate those values? How do you hold the organization to those values?

▶ What does success look like for your organization? Can you define it?

▶ Does your team feel the same way about success? How do they define a successful day or week?

▶ Once you define success, how can you communicate it daily, weekly, monthly, quarterly, and annually?

CHAPTER 5

CADENCE

MY DOCTOR LOOKED AT ME and said, "You are too fat and too old to keep running like this." The news was not something I wanted to hear. I had come in with pain in my back, the type of pain that keeps you awake at night. At times, I could not even bend down to tie my shoes. As I sat there on the exam table with the crunchy white paper underneath my backside, I had been hopeful for a solution to my problem.

I had never been a great athlete. The athletic genes in my family seemed to have been distributed a little unequally in my opinion, and for some reason, everything became a little extra hard for me. But as I got older and my middle got a little wider, I started to run and found joy in running in a physical, emotional, and spiritual sense. But as with anything in my life, I needed a goal, something to aspire to, to stay motivated to run. Each year, our community hosts the 25K

(15.5 miles) United States National Championship race with elite runners from around the world coming to participate. Do not worry; this is not a story about me becoming an elite runner and winning a national championship. Finishing was my goal.

As I sat in the tiny antiseptic-scented exam room, I was in the middle of training for my thirteenth 25K—at the age of fifty. For most people, finishing the race once is an achievement; I was making it an annual event (much to the chagrin of my wife sometimes). But after miles of training for my thirteenth event, my back was killing me. My doctor looked at me and told me in an amused tone, "Thirteen is an unlucky number. Your racing days, especially the long races, are over."

I had a choice to make as I walked out of that room and headed to the check-out station: be done or continue to run. As I walked to my car, with my back still aching, I decided right then and there that in fact I was going to keep running, and I would run even more. Yep, that was exactly what I was going to do. In fact, I set a goal not only to keep running the annual 25K race, but also to run ten marathons (26.2 miles) in my fifties. I would show my doctor that in fact I was not too fat or too old.

With many people, setting a goal like this is easy, but actually doing it was extremely hard. I did not get much encouragement from many people around me. Most told me I might be able to do one marathon, but I would never do ten, especially in my fifties. But I also had an amazing family who encouraged me to believe in myself and find a way (with plenty of sacrifices by them along the way).

In fact, I did do ten marathons in my fifties. I actually finished ten marathons by the time I was fifty-five, five years earlier than planned. As I write this book, I am on my way to twenty-plus marathons. I even ran the Grand Canyon from the north to the south rim in an unsanctioned race. At my next doctor's appointment, let us just say I left my doctor speechless.

You may be thinking what an athlete who runs marathons has to do with running a business or even creating enterprise value. You will be surprised.

I was running one of my first marathons. Marathons typically have an early start, and this one was no different with a 6 a.m. start time. The sun had not risen yet, but the light was breaking over the horizon and highlighting the start sign. Nerves were high for me, as always. Questions swirled in my mind about whether I would even finish. As I started, putting one foot in front of the other, my pace per mile was all over the place, from nine minutes to eight to ten. I would pass and be passed by the same people. Frustration was setting in. I was never going to hit my goal time, so just a finish was enough. The sun was rising and so was my anxiety.

If you have never run a marathon, there is an entire science to running these 26.2-mile races. Inconsistent, too fast, or too slow running paces ultimately lead to some disappointing results. Don't just take my word for it. Watch marathoners at about mile twenty or twenty-two, and you will start to see the train wrecks. Trust me, I have been there and done that! Cadence in running is huge in terms of results, and I hadn't yet found mine for that first marathon.

My youngest daughter caught the running bug after my first marathon. She has become an amazing runner. In fact, I would call her a running beast. It has always been a blessing to run with my daughter, and for my early races, we started and finished together. But I always knew Father Time would catch up with me, and she would get faster.

As she progressed on her running journey, she developed a strategy through trial and error on what worked best for her. One of the keys to her success was a consistent running cadence. She would run approximately the same pace per mile, mile after mile.

In boating terms, I call it "getting up on plane." When boats are "up on plane," they are running in the most efficient way. If you want to run in an efficient manner to maximize everything in your body, a steady, almost rhythmic run is the key. It is doing the same thing over and over, the same pace per mile.

Her running efficiency and running effort at a consistent pace seemed almost effortless to me (if running 26.2 miles can be called effortless), and the results were amazing. In her last several marathons, she posted personal best times, and she is within minutes of qualifying for the Boston Marathon. The key for her—and eventually for me—was cadence, and this concept can translate from a racecourse to the boardroom.

Once you understand your Why, have your leadership in place, and have a common language with your values defined, the next C in the entrepreneurial journey is cadence. According to Merriam-Webster, cadence is a regular beat or rhythm. The key words in that definition are regular and rhythm.

A successful business is not a sprint, but a marathon. Of course, you will have some projects that require a sprint mentality, but in the macro world of business, it is a long-distance run.

What does corporate cadence look like? Most of you do it in some way, shape, or form, but I would challenge you to do it with purpose. Establish well-defined and meaningful meetings for each respective group on a consistent basis, with a heavy emphasis on consistent.

What does this actually look like? I will share an example involving our project manager team (though we did a version of this with all of

> Once you understand your Why, have your leadership in place, and have a common language with your values defined, the next C in the entrepreneurial journey is cadence.

our teams). Our project managers are the major link between our sales team and our technician team, and they ultimately deliver the ending project to the customer. We would meet on a bi-weekly basis with each project manager and review current projects, staffing requirements, projects to be invoiced and/or closed, etc., along with any open issues and concerns. One of the keys to sound corporate cadence is to use the same data and format each time. The data and format can evolve over time, but a consistent meeting looking at consistent data produces consistent results, otherwise known as corporate cadence.

I can hear some of the naysayers already grumbling about having another meeting. I am completely against meeting for the sake of meeting. Teammates should absolutely hate meetings with no direction, desired outcome, purpose, or structure, and you should too.

If you are unsure if the meetings are truly valuable, ask a teammate. I will give you a stark warning though. If you are doing your meetings well, with well-defined structure and the same data review each time, you will increase the accountability of the entire team and individuals. If you ask a person who hates structure and, most importantly, accountability, they will hate these meetings.

But guess what? That type of person is a drain on your organization. This process with defined values, clear definition of success, and regular reviews/meetings that reinforce those items with consistent data and purpose creates an atmosphere for success and gets rid of the teammates (using that term loosely) who do not want to be accountable for the results. I have been insulted by so many people who absolutely hate this process, but those people are the non-performers. This process helps you release them to another position that fits their skill set, or they end up leaving of their own accord. But the teammates who embrace this regular accountability will elevate their performance. As the old saying goes, a rising tide lifts all boats.

While regular reviews will vary for each department in terms of frequency and type of data, establishing a corporate calendar with these meetings in place is a powerful tool. If running too fast or too slow is frustrating you, I would challenge you to look at your corporate cadence. Do your meetings have a purpose? Are they consistent, and do you look at the same set of facts each time?

Remember to pace yourself, use a common language, and develop a cadence toward success. Engage your teammates and define what items you should be reviewing at each meeting (while this can evolve over time, I caution you to avoid "flavor of the day" data that is in one day and gone the next). Define your meetings, and ask for input on how your meetings can be successful.

Pace yourself, use a common language, and develop a cadence toward success.

In my business, I would have a standup meeting with the sales team every Monday morning. The advantage of standup meetings is that they are short and to the point. Nobody, including me, wants to stand for more than fifteen to twenty minutes. My sales team absolutely hated having these meetings first thing Monday morning, which were required with few exceptions (such as vacation, illness, or travel to see a customer). But what was the purpose of a Monday morning standup meeting? Was it punishment for those often-late teammates who couldn't quite get to the office by 8 a.m.? Of course not.

For those short fifteen minutes, we would review the previous week's results (remember, consistent data), give out a "big dog" award for the top-selling salesperson for the week (a revolving trophy of a huge dog bone), and do a go-round in which each person got two to three minutes to talk about the previous week and what was going on for them in the current week. They would also share any current issues they may have had. (Warning here: The goal was not to have anyone save up issues to be handled in this once-a-week meeting but to highlight any current issue they may have been facing.)

The process got the entire team, along with me, on the same page every week. I could communicate any corporate-related messages, review our current progress to our goals, and listen to my teammates chart out their courses for the week. We all got on the same page. You can harness the power of a standup only if you do it regularly (cadence) and with data (common language).

A funny thing happened after I sold the business. I assumed that since I was the driver of such a meeting, and the sales team hated those 8 a.m. Monday standups, as soon as I was gone, the meetings would stop. Guess what? Those meetings are still happening today, and the team is even more successful than before. That's the power of cadence.

I have one consulting client whose entire business is done virtually, and everyone works remotely. While this is a new reality for many companies, the challenges are still the same. How does he keep everyone on the same page? His answer was a thirty-minute daily check-in at the same time each day.

The team starts the day together, reviews current open items or issues, then goes out and executes. Since his business is network security, a daily check-in is critical for his customer base. He has a once-a-month meeting to review data, metrics, and progress to annual goals. These meetings, along with an annual corporate meeting to review the prior year and set direction for the current year, mean his team is almost always on the same page.

He adds a bi-weekly management review of his key metrics with his leadership team to make sure they are tracking both leading and lagging indicators (more on this in a future chapter), and his team is hyper-focused. He does not overkill the company with meetings but has found a way to establish a cadence that works for the team and keeps the team focused.

His customers are extremely happy, and he has seen his top-line and bottom-line results more than double in just a couple of years, and hence his exit value has increased significantly. Again, the power of cadence. Every company is different and may need more or less of a meeting schedule than this example, of course.

The power of cadence also reinforces those items we discussed in previous chapters. When you talk about values and use common language in your meetings, a building effect happens with your team. You move more like a singular organization with a singular purpose rather than an organization made up of several individuals with several different agendas. Your effectiveness increases exponentially, and your results will follow. Whether you have one hundred employees or only a few, the power of cadence is an essential building factor for your company and team.

NEXT STEPS

▶ What are the key corporate meetings you need to have on a regular basis? Ask yourself:
  - ▼ Why do you need the meeting?
  - ▼ What is the desired outcome of the meeting?
  - ▼ What do attendees wish to get out of the meeting?

▶ What are the key department meetings you need to have on a regular basis?
  - ▼ Why do you need the meeting?
  - ▼ How often do you need to meet to be effective (the goal is not to have meeting overkill, but to meet with a purpose)?
  - ▼ What format should the meeting be and what data do you need to review at each one?

▶ How does the leadership team hold each other accountable for these meetings?

CHAPTER 6

CULTURE

WAS BONE TIRED. It was that type of tiredness that made even my toes hurt. The clock showed 6:55 p.m. I picked up my cell phone, called the pharmacy, and asked very politely if there was any chance they could stay open until 7:05 p.m. "I will be there in ten minutes," I promised. The person on the other end of the phone told me in a matter-of-fact voice, "No, I need to be out of here at 7."

My day had started in the intensive care unit at the children's hospital. My youngest granddaughter, age two, was on her second day in the ICU after surgery for scoliosis in which doctors put two screws into her lower back. Addyson, or Addy for short, has had quite the journey for being only two years old. She was born with several issues, from an unattached esophagus to a hole in her heart to scoliosis to lung issues. She had three major surgeries before she was six months old, and she had code blue three times in those early months.

The doctors wanted to wait until she got a little older to tackle the back issue. She had gotten through the four-hour surgery well, coming off the ventilator much better than previous surgeries, and we were in the process of moving from the ICU to a regular room. Because she was only two years old, her parents took twelve-hour shifts to make sure her needs were taken care of and address any issues that arose.

However, two-year-olds do not take well to a hospital stay. Despite the hospital staff's best efforts, getting a rambunctious two-year-old to sit still in a bed was impossible. To make matters worse, little Addy knew every time a nurse or someone she did not know came into the room, something uncomfortable was going to happen. The poor little girl would scream when these unannounced visitors showed up.

We had transitioned her to a regular room, and all she wanted to do was get out of it. The room to her meant discomfort, and getting out of the room was perceived safety to her. The hospital was designed in a circular fashion, with rooms on the outside and the nurses station in the middle. The walls were covered with colorful artwork. The ratio of staff to patients was high due to the young age of patients. But Addy wanted one thing: out.

Because she was recovering from back surgery, she was in a removable brace that minimized movement in her back and kept her left leg locked at a right angle. Between her and the weight of the brace, she weighed thirty to thirty-five pounds. Again, Addy wanted out. The brace could not come off. The next best solution was to take her out of the room in her pink brace and awkwardly hold her in front of you and start to walk. As we carried her out of the room, her anxiety eased.

Her mom (my daughter) is an amazing person, overcoming cancer at age twenty and going on to be a senior leader at her organization. She was the first to start carrying Addy around the circular floor. As I walked next to her, I could see the strain on her from lack of sleep, worry, and the sheer weight of her daughter and the brace. She took several laps around, then it was my turn. I pride myself, perhaps delusionally, as being strong and invincible even at my age, but carrying that weight around and around the circular hospital floor was exhausting. Addy and I would stop and look at the colorful pictures on the wall. She loved the ones of the animals the best. But every time I would try to sit down in the waiting area, she wanted to move. Maybe she thought if we were moving, they were not going to catch her.

As the day ended, I headed home, and my watch showed me that I had walked almost six miles that day, walking around the hospital with my recovering granddaughter. I was bone-tired, and I needed a break. All I was asking for from the pharmacy was five minutes.

I tried explaining to the person on the phone that my wife had been sick for weeks, we had finally got an antibiotic prescribed, and I wanted to get the medicine into her system as fast as possible. She politely told me she needed to leave right at 7 p.m. and I could pick up the prescription the following day. While I try to give people the benefit of the doubt—maybe she had a critical appointment or a family crisis or a plane to catch—but by the sound of her voice, I could tell I was just an inconvenience, a potential interruption to the end of her day. I would probably use an impolite word at this point, but I will be kind and say I was really upset.

Whose fault was this example of extremely poor customer service? The obvious first answer is the person on the phone whom I was trying to convince to stay open for 300 more seconds. Believe it or not, I don't blame this person. I, in fact, blame the leadership of the organization for creating this type of culture.

This type of scenario would have played out very differently at my company. Our culture was so customer-centric, that if any of our teammates had encountered this type of situation, not only would they have stayed open for the extra five minutes, but they would have tried to deliver the prescription to the customer. We were driven, and we were hyper-focused on creating a truly exceptional customer experience.

Changing culture starts with the leaders.

How do you change a culture? You need the items from the previous chapters, but above all, it starts with the leaders. It truly starts with the leader at the top. I did not inherit an anti-customer company, but I also did not inherit a customer-centric, driven company with teammates who felt valued.

I knew I needed to lead by example. I needed to show the team customer-centric leadership as well as let them know I valued them. One of my first experiences of leading by example in delivering for a customer was an installation that did not go exactly as planned. We were installing equipment for a customer in a pole barn that had no electrical power, but our equipment required electricity. We needed to dig a trench to bring the electrical line from the main house to the pole barn. We had given the customer a scope of work, noting that trenching may damage some of the landscaping, but we would do our best to minimize any damage.

The team did a great job with the trenching, but unfortunately, we were not able to work around a flowering pear tree, which we ended up damaging. The customer knew the risk because we had defined it ahead of time, but he was not happy. I saw this as an opportunity. The project manager of the job was ready to move on. In his mind, we did our job to the scope of work, and it was time to close out the project. I told him to give me a day, and I would take care of the customer. The project manager was a little befuddled, wondering what I was going to do and being completely unsure what he was supposed to do.

The next day, I jumped into my old red truck (remember Clifford?) and headed off to a nursery at a local landscape company. I was wearing a pair of old jeans, a grungy shirt, a ball cap, and a pair of work boots. A little rain was coming down when I arrived at the nursery. I asked the staff for help finding the biggest flowering pear tree I could fit in my truck and handle on my own. I ended up finding a beautiful seven-foot flowering pear tree and loaded it into my truck along with a shovel and several bags of topsoil. The rain started to get heavier and steadier.

The drive was about forty-five minutes from the nursery, and the rain increased to a deluge (not biblical proportions, but it was close). A passing thought entered my mind of trying on another day. The customer did not know I was coming, so twenty-four hours would not have made a difference. But I knew another twenty-four hours of a customer being disappointed was not the answer, so I continued my quest to his home.

His home was off the beaten path, accessible only by dirt roads and a dirt driveway, but it had a beautiful view of an inland lake. By the time I arrived, the dirt road and driveway had turned to a sea of mud. I exited my old red truck, and I started the process of finding the place where the old tree had been removed and putting the new one in a nearby spot. I got the tree out of the truck successfully, but the weight of the tree and the slippery ground caused me to fall. I gently slid down the steep slope of the driveway. The rain continued to pour, and I made another quick decision, which the customer appreciated.

Instead of planting the tree in a potentially wrong spot and risking electrical shock if I did cut the electrical line, I placed the tree with the dirt and the shovel underneath the overhang of the garage with note wrapped in plastic to keep it dry. The note was an apology to the customer. I headed back to the truck caked in mud from head to toe.

Instead of heading home to shower and change, I headed to the office. I wanted the team to see not a herculean effort by me, but an example of going the extra mile for a customer. The team was used to seeing me always dressed in a more formal way, since most of my day was spent seeing customers. When I arrived with dirt and mud all over me, they were more than surprised. But the lesson was clear: We take care of our customers. It was the first step of many in building a great culture centered around our customers and our teammates.

Torben Rick wrote a great short article titled "How and Why Organizational Culture Eats Strategy for Breakfast, Lunch, and Dinner."[8] His thoughts are timeless, and I simply cannot improve upon his insights:

> "Culture eats strategy for breakfast," a phrase originated by Peter Drucker and made famous by Mark Fields, (former) President at Ford, is an absolute reality! Any company disconnecting the two is putting their success at risk. However, while many studies show there is a direct correlation

between a healthy, productive culture and a company's bottom line, the majority of companies spend little time thinking, let alone doing anything about, this topic—even when they are spending lots of time thinking about their business strategy.

If you are following the process in the book, you have defined your Why, you have built your leadership team, developed a common language (avoiding the Tower of Babel syndrome), and built some cadence into your organization. Developing or even changing a corporate culture is one of the most challenging tasks you can accomplish, and most organizations do it by accident.

The owner or leader of the business wakes up one day and wonders how the company culture got to its current state, and if it is bad, they look everywhere but where the blame belongs: on the owner or the leader! If you are unwilling to take responsibility and take the lead on your organizational culture, stop! You need to put this book down and look in the mirror and think about who owns and is responsible for your culture. If you are unable to own your culture, you will never put all the pieces together and maximize your exit.

I bought my company in 2007, right before the Great Recession. The company I bought was a small organization of less than forty people and made about $9 million in sales.

The interesting thing is, the company intentionally capped its sales volume, and over several years, it never exceeded the $9 million mark. While that was clearly an ownership decision, the effect on culture was powerful. The previous owner may not have realized what he was doing, but the company I took over was very different from the company I wanted. The owner capped sales because he wanted a "lifestyle company." This is not a bad decision, and every owner needs to decide what type of company they want, but if you want a lifestyle company, you will never maximize the potential value of your company. I also believe by being a lifestyle company, you do your employees a huge disservice.

> If you are unable to own your culture, you will never put all the pieces together and maximize your exit.

I had a very humbling experience with my own team. We had reached a great level of success, had a very talented leadership team, had defined our values, shared the same definition of success, had a common language, and had a strong corporate cadence. So, guess what I did? This ranks up there as really stupid. I told the team in one of our regularly scheduled leadership meetings that I was done growing the business. I wanted essentially a lifestyle company.

The looks on the faces of my leaders were not what I expected. My general manager spoke up and stated clearly that while he could not speak for others, if the business was going in that direction, he would be leaving the organization. He was immensely proud of what we had built, the progress and results we were achieving, and all of a sudden, I was putting on the brakes. Not one of my leaders disagreed with him. I had hired some talented, driven leaders, and I just told them to stop growing. It was the same disease my predecessor had only at a different level.

There is an old saying that when you stop growing, you die, which can be true for about any aspect of life. I had just told my leadership team that the business was going to die. I reflected on my decision (and I did not take too long). Then I pulled my leadership team together and told them very humbly that I was wrong. I wanted to continue to invest in the company and more specifically in them and our team-mates. Our future was going to be even brighter, I promised.

When I sold the company a few years later, the acquiring firm (a multibillion-dollar company) told us we were the best acquisition they had ever made. We were an extremely well-run company with an amazing culture. While many companies go backward after selling to a bigger organization and the owner goes away, my company has continued to grow, and many of the leaders have taken on newer responsibilities in the much larger organization.

So, what is a lifestyle company? A lifestyle company is just like it sounds; it is about the employees' lifestyle. Work is viewed as an interruption of the employees' lives. How does this manifest itself in the workplace? I call it the "soft forty club." Workers do not work a full forty-hour week. If you have a company with no goals, no metrics, no vision (other than no growth), then you are going to get a large amount of your employee base working "soft forties."

While we had some employees who were dedicated and worked the necessary hours to get the job done, a large section of our base were the lifestyle employees. Those employees were the ones who could not find a way to work even close to forty hours, though they earned a salary based on forty hours or more. They were never in early or on time, always found a way to leave early in the afternoon, and almost never worked on Friday afternoon. Our organization took on the work ethic of the previous owner. Keep in mind, this is not a criticism of a choice to be a lifestyle company, but your choice on the type of company you are or want to be has consequences.

Another aspect of culture is the personality of the organization, which reflects the owner's personality. Most owners have a strength, some technical or operational focus, such as finance, human resources, sales, marketing, engineering, etc. There is no "right" personality for your company, but you need to recognize it, maximize it, and place key people in those areas where you are weak.

The company I acquired took on the personality of the owner from a technical standpoint, and the focus and strength of the company was primarily on the technical side. There is no danger in being a strong technical company and having that be the personality of the company. That said, if you neglect the other areas, you become very one-sided, and the other areas atrophy.

I came to the organization with a strong finance background. In many cases, this draws raised eyebrows. The talk among the team centers on beliefs like "going to gut the place," "all about the numbers," and "turn and burn." While finance was my strength, and the company's strength at that point was operational, my goal was to develop a different type of personality. I made the decision that our personality would be based on our Why—We value people—which includes our customers and the entire customer experience, from the initial meetings to the final installation to service and support. We also believed our Why included our teammates, vendors, and stakeholders. It was very challenging to move from an operationally based company to a customer-centric one (and dispel the rumors of a finance-driven company) and live out our Why.

Keep in mind, transition takes time. Sometimes it takes years depending on the amount of change required. It takes time to build up trust, and some teammates never get there because of all the baggage from previous years.

For example, when I sold the business, I still had some legacy teammates waiting for the other shoe to drop, even though they had more than tripled their individual income over the previous twelve years and were given more opportunities to grow not only financially but also personally and professionally. There was too much "old stuff" in their memory banks.

So, where does it start? It starts with you and then your executive and leadership team (hence the need to get those positions right before you focus on culture). You must engage, you must get involved, and you must lead. You must set the tone, establish the cadence, and be hyper-focused on building your culture.

While working hard and being driven were important at my company, a strong work-life balance was also a key for us. We tracked overtime hours, not to keep track of costs, but to keep track of the work-life balance. If we saw a teammate working too many hours, we would step in and figure out a way to get their work-life balance back in alignment. Because work-life balance was so important, we would review overtime every week to make sure we were keeping our fellow teammates healthy in all aspects of their lives.

You must build upon your desired culture. For us, if it was valuing people, then I needed to know my fellow teammates and know our customers, vendors, partners, and stakeholders. My team did too. It takes time to get to know someone, and I don't mean through a spreadsheet or an email or a text message. I mean real, face-to-face engagement.

> **You must set the tone, establish the cadence, and be hyper-focused on building your culture.**

In today's day and age, this is "anti-technology," but this is the best way to value people.

I did a lot of walking around and listening to my teammates and customers. I found out their hopes, dreams, and fears. We did silly things which became corporate traditions, and do not underestimate the value of tradition. These corporate traditions reinforced our values and created a culture of letting our teammates know they are valued, which ultimately led our teammates to value our customers with an exceptional experience.

Some of these traditions may seem silly in today's world, but they bound us together as an organization. This may seem redundant, but our traditions also followed a cadence, something our teammates could count on every year.

One of the traditions I kept alive (and tried to improve upon) from the former owner was our annual technician breakfast where the non-technician team would cook and serve our front-line technicians. As we grew this endeavor, it became a little more challenging to serve up breakfast to more than forty-five teammates. But this tradition, as

> Corporate traditions can reinforce your values and create a culture the lets your teammates know they are valued, which ultimately leads to an exceptional experience for your customers.

simple as it may have been, bound us an organization and created a one-team environment.

Another tradition we started, and one of my favorites, was a Christmas tradition. The Sunday before Christmas Eve, my wife and I would fill custom-made, company-blue stockings for each teammate and hang them by their office or workplace. We put traditional Christmas stuff in the stocking along with a gift and some Christmas cash. Blue stockings hung all over the office and warehouse. On Christmas Eve, we would close the office at noon, have a catered lunch for everyone, play games (I always wanted to be a game show host), and give away prizes.

But as much as the team enjoyed receiving, they loved the community give-back events we did every year. Along with collecting Christmas gifts for those in need in our community, we would do community projects together, such as adopting families around the holidays, placing wreaths on graves for our veterans, or volunteering at the local arena to raise money for those less fortunate in our community. Every event was met with enthusiasm and engagement from the team. It was never a requirement or expected, but the generosity of the team always amazed me, and it reflected one of our values.

One of the unintended benefits of building such a strong, positive culture was that the company became a desired place that individuals wanted to come to and work. We had become one of the best companies in the area because of our culture. When the firm who eventually bought the company saw what we had created, their response was, "We better not screw up the culture; this is the secret sauce of this company." I am proud to say that even though it has been a few years since the acquisition, the culture that was built still survives today.

What does your culture look like? Is it what you want? How would your teammates assess your culture? As owner and leader of your company, you are the "culture czar." While changing culture is truly a long game, sometimes taking five to seven years to effectively make a significant change, once you do it and continue to reinforce and build upon it, the results and momentum will amaze you. Culture truly does eat strategy for lunch.

NEXT STEPS

- ▶ Assess your culture with your leadership team in a candid and honest manner.
  - ▼ Does your culture align with your stated values?
  - ▼ What don't you like about your current culture?
    - ▶ What do you need to do to change it? How?

- ▶ Consider your corporate traditions.
  - ▼ Are they haphazard or done with a purpose and on a regular basis?
  - ▼ Do your traditions align with your stated values?
  - ▼ What new traditions should you try (and it is okay to fail)?

- ▶ Engage others in helping you build the positive culture and traditions you would like.
  - ▼ For each community outreach project we did at my company, a different teammate led the effort.

CHAPTER 7

ACCOUNTABILITY AND NUMBERS

I LOOKED ACROSS THE table and asked him, "So, where is your business going?" We sat in a small, beautifully designed conference room with a lot of windows. It was one of those beautiful late fall days with crisp cool air outside and bright sunshine streaming into the room. The setting was perfect for a little one-on-one meeting with this talented entrepreneur. He had built a couple of businesses from scratch, but his current business had plateaued. In fact, as we looked under the hood, we found the business was struggling to gain traction. He looked a little confused and wondered if the question was rhetorical. I asked it again a little differently, "Do you know where you are going, and how do you know when you get there?"

He answered me with a sharp tone, "I will know when we get there."

I asked, "Okay, I will give you that, but when will your team know?"

I could see the question swirling in his head. In an even sharper tone, he told me, "When I tell them."

At that point, I was clearly at the point of agitating him, so I went a little different direction with the ultimate intent still in mind. I asked in an even tone, "If you will know when you get there, tell me where the business is today."

He perked up. At last, a question he knew he had the right answer to. He grabbed last month's financial statements, tossed them my way, and calmly said, "Here. This is where we are right now."

I knew my next question was either going to make or break our discussion. I looked at the financial statements then at him. "These statements are three weeks old. I asked where you are today." I knew that was the moment he was either going to buy in or throw me out.

His expression became more pained. He said, "You know what? I think you might be onto something. I am not exactly sure where we are today, and to be honest, I am not exactly sure where we are going or if we are even getting better." He finally relented. "I think I need some help."

It took a while, but I got him there. I got him to think about his business differently. Most entrepreneurs are exactly in or pretty close to this same situation. They manage the business by feeling, more of an art than a science, and have the business run them versus them running the business.

I was feeling a little relieved that I had gotten him to that point, because there could have been a version where it might not have ended well. I told him, "Let's build a business GPS, which will help us understand where we have been, know where we are, and have an idea as to where we are going."

> **Most entrepreneurs have the business run them versus them running the business.**

He exclaimed, "I am all in!"

A "business GPS" is an essential element all businesses need.

At this point, you have done some serious heavy lifting. You understand your Why, have built your leadership team, developed some common language and cadence, and established a strong culture. If you have done those items—and those are some serious items—you should be congratulated on your progress. It is now time to really get serious and leverage those efforts.

You may have already seen an uptick in your business. The business feels better, and you are building a great company. Remember, people buy great companies for serious money. But we are not quite there yet; we are close, but not there.

Most of us today use some kind of navigational app to get us to our destination. The apps are usually cool, giving us a map view of where we are, an expanded view of the entire course, data along the way, estimated travel time, and estimated arrival time. Some apps even give you even more detail along the way, such as traffic slowdowns, stalled vehicles, or even police presence. All apps give you information along your route to let you know how you are doing. Many of us especially rely on our navigation system to get to places we have never been before.

What is funny (or sad, depending upon your point of view) is we use this type of process to get us from Point A to Point B, but so many of us hesitate to use this type of process in our businesses. Why? For some, it is because numbers can be intimidating or confusing. But the world revolves around numbers, whether we like it or not. You cannot hide from them. Numbers exist wherever we go, impacting almost everything we do, yet so many of us are resistant to running our businesses with numbers in mind.

I have heard hundreds upon hundreds of excuses, because business owners do not want to deal with the numbers. In fact, business owners will hire consultants who build wonderful and elaborate strategic plans costing thousands of dollars but will never get down to the numbers on how to make sure they will get there. Word of wisdom: If your consultant is not talking about the numbers and how to use them to track your progress on a regular basis, run away and run away fast, or just be ready to empty your checkbook.

I have been insulted, laughed at, and criticized by so many business owners, employees, and consultants because of my passion for numbers. My favorite one was this: "Because you are a finance guy, you like numbers." Really? That line is the ultimate cop-out. The world runs on numbers, and you better understand your business numbers to create a great company.

The reason business owners, employees, and all those high-priced consultants with their glossy strategic planning books don't like numbers is because numbers do a couple of things which everyone in business needs. First, they tell you if you are on the right path. If you

If your consultant is not talking about the numbers and how to use them to track your progress on a regular basis, run away and run away fast.

are checking your progress every ninety days, you are too late! You need to know as soon as possible if you are going in the wrong direction. The other reason and the biggest reason people dislike numbers is accountability. If I commit to a number or set of numbers, I really will know if I am succeeding or not. This is why so many owners, employees, and consultants run away from tracking progress—it makes them accountable.

Let's say you are struggling with weight. The numbers naysayers will tell you not to get on a scale, or if you must get on a scale, do it every ninety days or so. This approach is a recipe for disaster, yet I see it day in and day out with businesses. They do not really understand their numbers, and if they are looking at their numbers, they are usually looking at numbers that are old and are a lagging indicator.

One of my business heroes is Alan Mulally, former CEO of Ford. He turned a company that was losing a tremendous amount of money ($17 billion) to profitability. How did he do it? He and his executives understood the numbers and the accountability that came with them. He was passionate about his line, "Data will set you free." This mantra became the mantra at Ford. And guess what happened? Positive results.

Opinions are like noses (or something else). Everyone has one, but there is only one set of facts (numbers). Data-driven decisions will outperform those gut-feeling or "I just know" decisions.

You know your business better than anyone. You know it inside and out. You know the strengths and weaknesses and should (and I emphasize *should*) know the key drivers to your business. But I would challenge you to consider if your team knows your numbers. Do you share with them on a regular basis? That sounds like cadence to me. Do they know what the numbers mean? That sounds like a common language. Do they know how to move them? That sounds like culture.

While it is critically important to understand your profit and loss statements and balance sheet, as these financial statements are the ultimate measuring points, it is also important to understand the numbers behind the financial statements. So many business owners don't. If you really understand your business, you will develop numbers or metrics that you can review on a daily, weekly, and monthly basis that drive the results in your financial statements.

At this point, many business owners reading this book are having either a migraine or a meltdown. The problem with traditional financial statements is they tell you where you have been and the strength of the company at a particular point in time. Unfortunately, these financial statements are like looking in the rearview mirror. Many business owners do not have even a basic understanding of their financial statements. If this is you, let me make this clear: You better have a basic knowledge of your financial statements or you will never build a great business. You may be the best salesperson, best engineer, or best whatever in the world with the most amazing product, but if you don't understand your numbers, you are doomed to a poor exit or worse. The bankruptcy courts are filled with business owners who did not know how they got there, and the sad fact is they did not understand their numbers.

If financial statements are looking in the rearview mirror, how do you look forward? Every business needs to look at

> **If you really understand your business, you will develop numbers or metrics that you can review on a daily, weekly, and monthly basis that drive the results in your financial statements.**

both lagging indicators and, more importantly, leading indicators. The latter are the indicators that tell you where you are going. Remember those navigational apps? Most of the time you are using it, it is figuring out whether you are still on track versus where you have been.

When I coach business owners, I give them a simple exercise. It is simple in terms of instruction, but in many cases, it is difficult to do. The instructions are straightforward. If you were isolated from your business for six months, what are the four to six measures or metrics you would need to know to tell how your business has done and where it is going? The only caveat is you cannot look at your financial statements.

Once you identify those key measures (and remember, they all cannot be historical), you should measure those numbers in some cases every week. I can hear the screaming: "Every week? I will not have time to run my business!" I promise this process helps you run your business. Once you start the process of reviewing those metrics with your team, you will eventually add more metrics in the process. The goal is to start small and engage others on your team in identifying and creating these metrics.

Do not try to measure everything. Major in the majors, and do not major in the minors. Identifying the key drivers of your business, looking at them week in and week out, and understanding the trends will keep your business from getting off track.

Back to the story I was telling at the beginning of this chapter. After hearing my prospective client exclaim, "I am all in," I took him through this simple but effective exercise. You are removed from your business for six months, and it is the first day, the first hour of your return. You have your cup of coffee. What six things do you want to know to understand where your business has been over the past six months and where it is going? Believe it or not, the answers came pouring out of his month. Without looking at financial statements, he told me he would like to know cash balance in the bank, current accounts receivable balance, sales backlog (orders not fulfilled), current sales pipeline (sales orders they were hoping to close), chargeable hours for his technical team, and average length of time a service ticket was open.

I said, "Perfect. Let's start tracking this data every week and review early in the week in case we need to address any issues."

He balked at first and said that while he would like to look at such data, it simply would take too long to gather up, and he did not have the time to do it. That was where my selling skills came into play. I convinced him to give it a month, and if he did not find it useful, then we could kill it and he could send me home. He took the challenge, and over the next four weeks, he collected the data, actually added more data points, and reviewed it with me each week. Over those four weeks, we found weaknesses in his processes, some underperforming employees, and the truth that the long-range forecast was not as promising as he had thought. Remember, his previous reference point was three-week-old financial statements.

After four weeks, it was time to either move forward with the process of gathering, reviewing, and improving metrics, or to toss the whole thing out because he initially said he did not have the time. I opened the meeting and said, "After thinking about the whole process of metrics, measurements, and reporting, let's toss the whole thing out and try something different." I call this tactic the takeaway.

He told me, "You are crazy! I have a much better understanding of my business. My leadership team has a much better understanding as well, and for the first time, we are on the same page. We have improved some items already along the way and identified other issues. I am sold."

Fast forward thirty-six months, he is truly running his business. His teammates are happier and more focused on what they need to do, and his profitability has increased by a factor of three. It works.

I have had clients with weeks' worth of data for years, and they look at the current week along with data from the previous weeks to help them know if they are on track or need a slight course adjustment. So, get out your Excel spreadsheets or another similar tool and start tracking your key metrics.

This exercise forces business owners to understand the true drivers of their business. I am a frequent viewer of *Shark Tank*. This is a great show where entrepreneurs who are usually in the early stages of their business pitch their company to a group of investors. The investors are people who have been successful in building great companies. If you ever watch the show, then you know that one thing is sure to happen: If you don't understand your numbers, you will get fileted. Some "sharks" on the show are nicer than others, but none of them will come near a business if the owner does not have working knowledge of the numbers of their business. One of the favorite metrics the sharks will ask for from those making their pitch is their cost of acquiring a new customer. I can tell you with certainty that the answer to this question is not a single line on your profit and loss statement, but it needs to be answered so you understand your current profitability. With direction, you can drive this cost downward, which means more profitability.

In my previous business, one of our biggest metrics was utilization rate. We were effectively a job shop. Every job was customer-specific, and more than half of our employees were front-line technicians. If our technicians were charge-able (hours charged directly to a job) at a high percentage compared to their total hours, then we knew we were on track. In fact, we built our utilization rate into our budget by technician, so we knew the financial impact of missing or achieving this metric. This metric was such a key for us, we reviewed it weekly, down to the technician level if neces-sary. When our utilization rate was strong, our profitability was strong. We did not have members of our team standing around, and the support team around them was efficient in keeping them chargeable.

Someone may ask, "Every week?" And my answer is, Yes, every week for your key numbers or metrics. If you want to be successful in your business, you must be hyper-focused on the right things. You must be driven to understand your numbers and make those numbers move in the right direction. Numbers or metrics create accountability. If you do not want to do this type of heavy lifting, if you want to be an absentee owner or just pick up your mailbox money, that is fine, but it will come at a cost upon your exit.

Another leading indicator for us was the number of quotes we produced per week. Over any given period, we knew our historical close rate of quotes, so our number of quotes produced gave us a forward-looking view. Quotes produced would give us an idea as to the types, amount, and quantity of deals, and when coupled with our close rate (which we would update), we could get a good idea as to the sales pathway of the business. Again, quotes produced did not show up in our financial statements, but it was a key indicator of where our business was going.

Move beyond the shoebox mentality of running your business.

Every business is different, but you must understand your revenue and cost drivers, both leading and lagging indicators, and track those results on a very frequent basis. If you cannot do this, I would challenge you to say that you do not know how your business works. You must move beyond the shoebox mentality of running your business, meaning you put all receipts and disbursements in a shoebox and hope you have something positive left over at the end.

Now is the time to get going and really understand your business. Start simple with metrics that are easy to measure, then track regularly. I recommend weekly with a monthly recap. This is *not* a static process. If you are doing it well, you will change and modify your metrics as you review them. This should drive more questions into the inner workings of your business.

My other suggestion is that once you have your metrics established, create a vehicle to communicate them with your team on a regular basis. This helps in a couple of key areas from the previous chapters. These metrics help everyone understand what drives the business (common language), and if you review the data, it creates cadence.

If you want to create a great company and not just a great business, then understand your numbers and spend time with your teammates to develop them together. You should build a one- or two-page report with all these metrics with historical data, current data, and targets. Most business owners end up with a hodgepodge of information in which they soon lose interest. Create this one- or two-page report, and review it on a regular basis (see the Appendix for an example template).

When done well, the metrics will be the glue that holds all your hard work together. You will know if you are getting off course or missing your strategic plan. You will know where you need to spend some time and energy.

Key reminder: Do not try to measure everything. Major in the majors, not in the minors. Develop a scorecard of these key measures, but do not measure the mundane and the irrelevant.

Now that you have your metrics in place, it is time to turn up the heat and make the company engine roar!

NEXT STEPS

▶ Start with your leadership team and have them independently write down the four to six metrics they believe are needed to tell where the business has been and is going.

   ▼ Once each leadership teammate has completed their list, accumulate the metrics and identify the ones with the most votes from the team.

   ▼ Once you have your initial metrics, start to chart them.

▶ Develop a schedule to share the data with your team.

   ▼ Some groups have a more frequent review than others (and sensitive information may be limited to specific groups).

   ▼ Once you start tracking the data, how do you move the metrics in the right direction? Tracking data for data's sake is worthless. Having the metrics make positive moves is the key.

NEXT STEPS (CONTINUED)

▶ Rinse and repeat.
  ▼ This is not a once-and-done idea. Always be looking for new ways to track your business that make sense. Over time you will settle on the needed metrics.

SPECIAL NOTE

Every business owner I have done this process with starts with kicking and screaming, but after several weeks of looking at the data, I ask the business owner what would happen if they stopped tracking the information. Everyone's reaction is the same: "No! This actually works."

In fact, one of my clients that was recently purchased shared the metric report with the private equity firm that bought the business, and the firm's response was to mandate the report for all of their companies.

IF YOU STICK TO IT, THIS WILL WORK!

CHAPTER 8

GASOLINE

MY TEAMMATE WAS a little reluctant to come into my office. After all, he was coming in with a big ask. His particular area of responsibility needed a capital infusion. He sat down in my office, looked at me a little sheepishly, and said he needed more money to make a necessary infrastructure improvement. Our network of servers was old, tired, and not up to date, and with the current ongoing risk of managing sensitive customer data and the everyday threat of cyberattacks, I knew he was right. But where was I going to get the money? To add more stress to the situation, he was not the first person to come into my office needing more money for their respective areas.

I was like most entrepreneurs. I did not have a lot of liquid personal financial wealth. My parents were far from rich. My dad had been a journeyman electrician, so I did not get a financial head start in life. My house was already mortgaged to the maximum along with any bank loans for the business. I was tapped out, but I needed access to capital. As I looked at the year ahead, I not only had to make an investment in the infrastructure of the business, but I also needed to give my teammates raises, cover medical insurance costs that had doubled in the past several years, and pay other increased operational costs. I had a real problem.

I evaluated my options. I could bring in some outside capital from other partners, but I would have to give up more equity along the way. I already had a 20-percent partner, and I did not want to lose more equity. So, outside capital was an expensive option. Another option would have been to go back to the bank.

They had loaned us both a long-term note and a short-term working capital loan along with a capital improvement loan. I felt going to them again would be a reach, but I thought it might be my only plausible option outside of bringing on another outside investor or selling more ownership to my existing investor. I needed more fuel for my business. I needed more gasoline to make this company really go.

This can be a frustrating place to be for an entrepreneur. You have your team in place, you have your common language and cadence, you have built a wonderful culture, and you understand your metrics and what drives your business. But you need fuel. You need cash to take the business to the next level. You may not believe me at this point, but this is a potential turning point for your business. This is truly the fun part of building your business, but this can give some business owners incredibly high anxiety.

Most business owners are control freaks. They are the super anal individuals who like to control everything. I hate to say it, because I was one also. I suffered so much from being a control freak, I would even shovel the sidewalks around our building sometimes because it was not done just right. While this is one of the reasons you are so successful, if you are going to grow your business and exit well, you need to build a company in such a way that you may feel like you are losing a little control. The gasoline you are about to pour on your business, however, will give you more control and fire up the engine.

One of my favorite sharks on *Shark Tank* is Kevin O'Leary. Mr. O'Leary sometimes plays the foil to the other sharks on the show, who are equally as astute and bright as he is. He has a great saying on the show that is so true (and it is not "you are dead to me," which he likes to say in response to a failed pitch). Mr. O'Leary says his money or investment is like gasoline on a fire—it makes it roar. Most of us will never make it on *Shark Tank*, so how do you make your business roar and take it to the next level without going to the bank and borrowing more money or remortgaging your home?

I cherish solving complex issues and taking risks. The capital problem I faced was no different. I had all the facts and context, but I needed to solve the issue or I was going to lose more of my company. So how did I do it?

Very simply: through variable compensation plans. Before you have a meltdown and yell and scream or throw the book across the room (or shut down the e-book), you need to think about what you have created. Now is the time to leverage that demanding work.

One of the greatest CEOs of all time, Jack Welch, the former leader of General Electric, made it very clear what compensation plans can do for you. He said, "If you pick the right people and give them the opportunity to spread their wings and put compensation as a carrier behind it, you almost don't have to manage them."

I have experienced this firsthand. If done well, your teammates will drive the right results (understanding your metrics is key here), which in turn will drive the right financial rewards both for the business and your teammates.

In my lifetime, I have created hundreds of variable compensation plans. I must admit reluctantly that I have built some horrible plans, but I have learned from those mistakes. I must give one warning here, and I am not trying to scare you. Just like gasoline, variable compensation

> **"If you pick the right people and give them the opportunity to spread their wings and put compensation as a carrier behind it, you almost don't have to manage them."**
>
> **—JACK WELCH**

plans can burn you badly, or they can accelerate your growth. Well-designed compensation plans are one form of capital you can employ in your business while managing the risk.

When I bought my business twelve years ago, there were zero variable compensation plans. The previous owner, if the year went well, would decide on an arbitrary number and divvy it up based on how he felt about each employee. Many, and I mean many, business owners do this, because they are in total control of the process. But the problem here is most employees end up disappointed. I have been on the receiving end many times.

The business owner, who felt he was generous, has an unhappy employee who most likely is not motivated for the future. The business owner did not get his money's worth. He did have complete control but with unintended consequences. So, what went wrong? It all comes down to one word: expectations. The employee expected one thing in terms of his bonus, and the owner delivered something else, even though the owner thought he or she was being generous. The sad part is everyone loses. How do you fix it? Simply set the expectations up front. At the start of your fiscal year, lay out your expectations as well as how the employee can make more money by meeting or exceeding those expectations. It is all about designing a variable compensation plan that drives your metrics.

Where do you start on building variable compensation plans? First, variable compensation plans are dollars available to an employee above his or her base which are conditional on some result or metric. There is that word again: metric! If you have done the last chapter well, this is the easy part. You link the variable compensation plans to some of your key metrics.

Twelve years ago, I started slow and with the easiest group of people first. Initially when I bought the business, salespeople got a base salary, and if the company did well, the owner may (and the word "may" is important) have given out a small bonus. If you had a great year but you somehow made the owner mad right before bonus time, guess what happened? Bad news for you. You may have had your discretionary bonus reduced or taken away altogether. How did the sales team react to this base pay plan plus maybe a bonus at the end? Some worked as little as possible but enough to avoid being fired. Some would call this "working smart." In terms of base compensation, there was zero difference between a high-performing salesperson and a low-performing one. In fact, the salespeople did not even have sales goals.

When building a variable compensation plan, start slow and simple. That's the number-one rule. The number-two rule is never, and I mean never, build a compensation plan that is too confusing to understand. You will not get your money's worth, trust me. I have built some super complicated plans that were utter failures. A complicated compensation plan may make you feel good, but they are a disaster! The KISS principle is key here (Keep It Simple, Stupid). Most compensation plans, if done well, should allow the teammate to be able to calculate in their heads the impact on their variable pay.

The KISS principle is key when building a variable compensation plan.

In my company, we paid the salespeople a percentage of the margin produced. That was really simple. The job was completed, all the revenue and costs were accumulated, and they received a percentage. We told them up front that their salaries would be frozen, and if they wanted to make more money, then they needed to sell more. For those who sold a lot more, they would make a lot more money. Guess what happened? Our salespeople drove more sales and more margin. In fact, some sales members saw their compensation double or triple, and there were a few more newer cars in the parking lot. Another funny thing happened. Those underperformers, who were no longer going to get a raise for just showing up, self-deported. This was truly a win-win scenario. We drove more sales with more margin and rewarded the teammates who got us there while the bad ones left.

We took the same approach over the years with almost every department. Remember the infamous metric of utilization rate from the last chapter? The better our utilization rate, the better the company ran, and the more money we made. Our project managers managed the day-to-day activity of the technicians, so we created a simple variable compensation plan for every percentage point they beat the targeted utilization rate (which was based on the budget). That was how they earned a bonus. Simple, safe, and effective. Every week, we would look at the utilization rate on the weekly level as well as the year-to-date basis, so the team knew exactly what the bonus level was.

These plans were easy to design and helped get the company to where it was, but I was still in a cash crunch. What was I to do? The solution I proposed was to grow our way out of the cash crunch and create more financial opportunities for the entire team.

One of the key metrics we looked at as a team every week and month was whether we had positive or negative slippage on our gross margin. Slippage is just like it sounds. It is the increase or decrease in expected margin on a specific job. Our company was essentially a job shop with every job being unique. Each job was quoted with a planned targeted margin. Once we started tracking slippage, we found a problem, a big problem. Our negative slippage over a two-year period exceeded $1 million. Put simply, we delivered as an organization $1 million less in margin than expected. For a business our size, that was a serious problem. But since we knew the numbers or metric, we knew fixing slippage would be the solution to our cash crunch. So, how did we fix it?

We created a variable compensation plan in which we gave each project manager a percentage of the savings on their individual jobs. If a job ran well and generated savings, the project manager would get a percentage of those savings. Conversely, if the job ran poorly and there was negative slippage, the same percentage was applied, and this amount was netted against any gains. When I presented this compensation idea to my leadership team, let us just say they thought I was crazy. We had limited cash reserves and a big slippage issue, and I was recommending giving teammates the opportunity to make more money. It was a rare moment in which I disagreed with my leadership team, and I told them to trust me that it would work. I had done something similar before on a much lesser scale with less risk, but it was time to go big or go home. As I reflect on all my decisions in business, that one was a tipping point for my company. I told my leadership team that it was a "burn the ships" moment. For context, "burn the ships" is a reference to the Spanish explorer Hernán Cortés who, upon arriving in Mexico in 1519, burned his ships to send a message to his men that there would be no turning back. We were not turning back either.

The project managers loved this plan. It was their business within a business. They were accountable to their results and were rewarded for it. Guess what happened to our slippage rate? It did a complete 180-degree turn. Instead of generating negative slippage, we generated positive slippage, generating more margin than expected. What did we do with the extra margin? We shared the margin directly with the project managers as it related specifically to their jobs. They were truly running their own businesses. They felt empowered, they felt in control, and they were rewarded for their performance. Even the sales team, which I noted before was paid on margin, loved this type of plan for the project managers because it meant higher margins for their jobs and hence higher commissions. We linked the sales team and project managers together with these types of compensation plans, and any silos within the organization soon disappeared. Our gross margins improved, teammates made more money, and the business was more profitable. The gasoline of the compensation plans made our company engine roar. And the company had more money for investment in the business, such as those infrastructure projects. We had grown our way out of the problem. The company was making more money, teammates felt a greater sense of empowerment and control, and they were making more money. Success bred more success.

I could go on and on about the various compensation plans we created. Each year, we would tweak them here or there based on our strategic initiatives, but the basic premise would stay the same.

Once you build the plans, one of the keys is to be completely transparent. If you create a plan and do not share the data, then skip creating plans altogether, because you will not get your money's worth. Depending upon the frequency of the payouts to our teammates, we created reports that detailed all the information that went into their variable compensation plans. Teammates must understand how the numbers are calculated so they can produce even more positive results. Do you know what happened to our teammates' expectations when it came to additional pay from the variable compensation plans? They were never disappointed. They knew the plan before the start of the business year, they understood how they could make more money, and the plans aligned with our metrics. Discretionary bonus plans are a lose-lose scenario. Variable compensation plans create winners across the board.

Once you build the variable compensation plans, one of the keys is to be completely transparent.

We continued to build variable compensation plans for almost the entire team. We rolled out each person's plan with a sit-down meeting. We reviewed the plan together and put a document in their hand that explained how the plan worked and the financial projections of their potential compensation. After the review was complete, all parties signed the document.

One more case study I will share involved our service department. We struggled for years to improve and grow our service department. Even though our installation footprint was growing, the overall profitability of the service department was flat or even declining. So, we decided to make a leadership change and put some real skin in the game.

We hired an exceptional candidate and gave her a compensation plan that gave her tremendous upside if we were able to hit our numbers. She crushed her numbers. In fact, the last two years I was owner, she hit her annual numbers by midyear. Because she made bonus dollars on every incremental dollar above the targeted plan, she made that department a major contributor to our bottom line. Service saw its revenue double while at the same time seeing its margin percentage double as well. This was a powerful combination. How did we do it? By putting the right metrics in place and creating a true compensation plan that rewarded (highly rewarded) great performance. This manager tracked results weekly, addressed issues in a timely manner, communicated performance with a weekly update, and made course corrections as needed. The results spoke for themselves. The compensation plan truly added gasoline to the service department results.

Most business owners are simply frozen when it comes to variable compensation plans. They are afraid of losing control or giving out too much money. Or, for some silly reason, they are afraid of the added accountability across the organization. I will tell you from experience, when we issued big bonus checks or big commission checks, it was because the organization got what it needed. In actuality, the company got even more. Meanwhile, the employee was thrilled with the check, and it motivated them to do even more.

We never set a ceiling on what employees could earn. I find it absolutely repulsive when compensation plans have a cap, and employees can make only so much. You do not have a cap on how much money you can make in your business, yet some business owners put a cap on compensation plans to their employees. Word to the wise, do not do it.

Any time an employee walked into my office asking to make more money, I very simply took out their compensation plan and reminded them of their unlimited earning potential. After a few of these visits, the number of employees coming to my office to discuss pay went to zero. A special note: It was always the underperformers who stopped in my office.

WORD TO THE WISE:

Do not put a cap on

compensation plans

for your employes.

One major thing to remember about variable compensation plans is to make sure you write them down in a formal format and give the employee a copy with signatures from both themself and their team leader. I have seen too many plans fail because they were not written down. Instead, the owner simply told the employee about how they were to be paid and provided no documentation. This is a huge failure filled with danger. If you do not write the plans down and share them with the employees, you are setting everyone up for unmet expectations. The formal process takes a little more work, but it is worth it. It solidifies the plans and sets the proper expectations.

If you want to take your company to the next level without going to the bank to borrow more money, build variable compensation plans. Start out small and simple (and always keep it simple), then share with your teammates how their numbers are calculated.

If done well, you will be amazed at the results. You will see superior performance by your team, which will garner great rewards for them and will drive a higher bottom line. This process also creates a further level of sophistication for your company, which makes it more attractive to potential buyers.

How did we do in my company after taking all the steps we have discussed so far? How did we do after making the changes in leadership, creating a common language, establishing a corporate cadence, defining a culture that valued our teammates and customers, setting innovative metrics, and introducing exciting compensation plans which rewarded everyone? We turned a small, flat-line business into one of the best companies not only in the industry but overall. We tripled our headcount, more than doubled our revenue, and tripled our bottom line while creating a culture that was the envy of many.

You can do it too. Take a courage pill, start with those baby steps, and put some gasoline onto the company fire!

NEXT STEPS

▶ Pick an area of your business that is easy to measure and aligns with your key metrics.

  ▼ Build a simple compensation plan for that area of your business.

  ▼ Track the results for a year then see where you need to make any changes.

  ▼ After one year, pick another area of your business, and rinse and repeat.

▶ If you already have variable compensation plans, consider the following.

  ▼ Do they follow the KISS principle?

  ▼ Are they written down and shared with the employee via their own individual copy?

  ▼ Do they align with your key metrics?

▶ Kill your discretionary bonus plans, and replace them with the plans outlined in this chapter. Every teammate should know how to make more money in advance of the business year. You need to get your money's worth, and discretionary plans are not the way. In fact, they are a waste of money.

CHAPTER 9

EXIT WELL

PULLED MY OLD, red truck into the lot of a well-manicured park. The park was one of those typical city parks, with a pavilion, a small play area for kids, and a couple of baseball fields. "No Golfing" signs were throughout the park. I looked around hoping no one would see me, then I closed my eyes and tried to drift off to sleep for a few minutes. I was a little embarrassed that in the middle of a workday I needed a break to take a nap. My rest breaks throughout the week were almost every day during lunch. Occasionally I would have a customer or prospect meeting during lunch time, which meant I would be exhausted by evening.

Business and life had taken a toll on me. I had purchased the business at age forty-six, gone through a business partnership transition that was hard on both of us, and endured the Great Recession all while leveraging everything I owned, which left me with no backstop. My wife and I had some unfortunate events affecting us personally as well. One of our children battled cancer, and right as we entered the empty nest phase, two nieces and a nephew came to live with us after their parents died in tragic ways.

Along the way, I had to manage a twenty-four-hour business. Many of our clients never shut down. They included hospitals, correctional facilities, and airports. When those clients called, we could not tell them we would get back to them at 8 a.m. I was the last one on the call list for twelve years. Even though in twelve years my phone only went off six times for an emergency, I had to always be vigilant no matter where I was or what I was doing. On top of those elements, I would work every weekend on planning and my weekly communication to the team. There was literally no downtime for me unless you count my marathon training, but even on those runs, I would take my phone and take calls if needed.

I had gone to see the doctor for a checkup because I was struggling with fatigue. I was a marathon runner; I should be in excellent shape. When the doctor called me, she told me I had a condition which caused chronic fatigue. She had never seen a blood work count so out of order. It was more than stress. I had an actual condition, and it would take time to heal. It was a tough moment for me. I thought I was invincible, that I could work longer and harder than anyone. In fact, one year I never took a vacation, worked seven days a week, and didn't take a dollar out of the business either in a paycheck or distribution (now that's stress).

The business had tripled in size, and we were continuing to grow. We had moved from a small business where people just wanted a job to a successful company where people wanted a career. I believed all along my entrepreneurial journey that I was simply a steward of something bigger than myself. The question facing me as a leader was whether I could take the team to the next level. Would I be a good steward?

One of the most underappreciated talents is knowing when to say it is time to be done. How many athletes have you seen who seem to hang on just a little too long? They long for one more home run, basket, or touch-down. They want one more game. But many stay too long. I heard a great saying once that a great legacy is built upon a great exit.

One of the most underappreciated talents is knowing when to say it is time to be done.

When it comes to knowing when to sell your business, it is a big decision. Perhaps that time has come for you. Any number of reasons have led you to decide to sell. Maybe you have had a good run and wish to move on to a new chapter in your life. Maybe health reasons or family reasons or some other personal reasons have prompted the decision to sell.

My human resource person came into my office late on a Friday afternoon. We were less than seventy-two hours from announcing the company had been sold. The all-team meeting was scheduled for 7 a.m. the following Monday. The transition team from the acquiring firm was flying in Sunday night, and I was scheduled to have dinner with them that evening. I was running on very little sleep and had been popping Dayquil pills for several days to stay awake, which I do not recommend. The final documentation was coming together, disclosure schedules were being finalized, terms and conditions were being put to bed.

She walked into my office and could see the tired expression on my face, one of sheer exhaustion. I was not even sure I could drive myself home that evening, but we were close to the end. We were close to a life-changing event for me and, most importantly, my teammates. She had that look on her face that said she had something she did not want to tell me. We had worked together for years, and I know I probably caused her more than one headache. I knew by her facial expression that whatever she had to say was not going to be good.

One of the key factors in all the meetings with the potential buyers was they were going to take care of the team first and foremost. This was always paramount in my mind. It did not matter how big of a check I was going to get if it came with a loss of jobs for my teammates. I am guessing this factor was deeply rooted in my upbringing and the layoffs my father endured throughout his working career and the subsequent impact on the family.

She had just completed a conference call with the human resources transition team from the acquiring company. She looked at me and said, "Five people are going to lose their jobs. They will be extended short-term employment contracts, and everyone else will get a long-term contract." I'm sure the color in my face, which was not great to begin with due to the lack of sleep and stress, became ashen. I had her take me through the conference call. Her answer was still the same: Five of my teammates were going to lose their jobs.

In the days leading up to finalizing deals, there is sometimes a disconnect between the dealmakers and the deal doers who get the deal closed. But somewhere between agreeing to terms with the dealmakers and the final documents, someone had decided that five of my teammates were no longer going to be employed.

I thanked my human resource teammate and told her I would take care of the situation. In hindsight, I probably did not handle that aspect of the transaction well, but sleep deprivation will do funny things to you sometimes.

I called up my business broker, who had done an amazing job in getting the company in front of the right people and navigating the deal process. This was going to be his most difficult challenge. I told him in a rather stern voice that the deal was off and to tell the transition team not to get on the plane on Sunday. Having five people lose their jobs was not part of the transaction. I was done. A sickening feeling must have fallen upon him, but to his credit, he told me he would get back with me. I told him it was not a negotiating tactic. They had twenty-four hours to put a proposal in front of me, and I would give them a yes or no answer.

There was a lot more drama in the following twenty-four hours that I will not go into details about, but my feeling on that Friday evening as I lay exhausted on my couch at home was that the deal was not going to get done. However, the acquiring company did come back with a solution that would work for me. Four out of the five people would receive long-term contracts, and the fifth person, who was on her way to retirement, would receive an extended retirement package (she thanked me later for the extra financial benefit). We were on our way to closing on Monday after a close call.

It is never an easy decision to sell your business. For some of you, this was a business you started or was a family-owned business. You have spent years, sometimes decades, building the company, and the emotional ties run deep. But as you think about selling your business, remember you are only a steward of the organization. While this approach may seem a little controversial, I believe it is true.

You are a caretaker. As a caretaker, you must make sure the business can go on to the next level. Remember, if you do not grow, you will eventually die. One of my reasons for selling the company was to make sure the company would have a future beyond me. While this may seem like a dark approach, we are all going to die someday, and how you leave your company is an important decision. I challenge you to think beyond yourself and be a good steward of the organization. I did not sell my business to an organization that gave me the most dollars; I sold the company to an organization that was the best fit. It actually drove my business broker nuts that I was less concerned about the money and more concerned about fit.

As you think about selling your business, remember you are only a steward of the organization.

If you have turned your business into a great company, then you have created enterprise value, and you have something to sell. If you have built a leadership team, a culture, an operational cadence, and a common language with metrics and processes, and you have layered variable compensation plans onto your corporate structure, you have probably seen some growth. Hopefully you have seen some explosive, profitable growth.

Companies love to buy companies that are growing. Companies love to buy companies that have a level of sophistication in their sales approach, their operations approach, and their customer service approach. I cannot tell you how many companies I talk with who cannot tell me what some of their leading indicators are when it comes to sales or other aspects of their business. Most of the time, I get a blank stare. Sophisticated businesses know the drivers of their sales and operations. These truths hold true no matter the size of your organization. Larger businesses may have a higher degree of sophistication, but all the elements discussed in this book hold true no matter the size of the business. Do these simple things, and your chances to sell your company for meaningful dollars is greatly improved.

The process of selling your business can take many forms, and it is not the purpose of this book (maybe a future book) to discuss the aspects of selling your business. Many people choose an investment banker, others a business broker, and others go through their business network. The purpose of this book is to help you maximize the value of your company.

Once you go through the process, decide to sell, and come to terms with the buyer, how you exit is so important.

The incoming company brings in a team to help with the transition and will move on-site for a period of time. One of the amazing facts I did not know was how many business owners simply send an email telling the employee base the company has been sold. I was absolutely dumbfounded at this approach. This is the Cowardly Lion approach (before he saw the wizard of Oz).

I decided to call an all-company meeting, which had a call-in option for anyone working remotely. I told everyone directly, in real time. It was one of the most difficult days of my life. I was filled with much emotion at saying goodbye to the company and the teammates I loved. But I knew full well I was placing them in good hands with more opportunity and a great future. When you sell, say goodbye in person. Your teammates helped build your company and should hear directly from you.

Also, share the proceeds. I issued my teammates checks that, combined, totaled more than seven figures. Could I have used the money, maybe for a big lake house? Yes, that may have been nice, but they helped build the company, and they deserved every dollar I shared with them.

I would also encourage you to be part of the transition team. I personally told key customers about the transition. I also stayed on for about six weeks to help with the transition, and I was not getting paid. A smooth transition was important to me to help the company move into the next stage.

Very simply, tell your team in person, share the proceeds (with some meaningful dollar figures), and help with the transition. Trust me, you will never regret it when you look back at your career. Remember a great legacy is built upon a great exit.

Exit well!

NEXT STEPS

▶ How are you going to tell your team about your exit?

▶ How much are you going to share with your team in terms of dollars?

▶ How much is needed/required for the transition from you? Remember, be helpful, but do not get in the way. You do not own the business anymore.

CHAPTER 10

FINAL THOUGHTS AND A LITTLE REFLECTION

"IT'S ONLY WORTH a quarter," my private equity partner said of my business with a little disdain on his face. He had come up to my office unannounced via the back stairwell, as he usually did on what seemed to be an almost daily basis. He was an extremely smart and talented individual, and his input, while difficult to hear at times, was usually filled with some sage advice. But that time was different.

Maybe it was my ego and pride, but his comment crushed me. He was not impressed with the direction of the business and, in effect, my ability to lead it. This was one of the most humbling yet pivotal moments for me in my business and my business career.

He told me my business (my baby, my blood, sweat, and tears) was worth less than 25 percent of when they bought in originally. The business, as with all businesses, was in a down-turn and had been performing poorly for about six months.

I must admit that I had taken my eyes off the business. I was not watching the leading and lagging indicators. I had a sales development hat on, and I missed my responsibility of being the owner. Simply put, I was letting the team down.

There is some dispute between the private equity partner and myself on exactly what he said, but I interpreted him as saying my business was not worth more than a quarter. Even though I was a little ticked off at what he had said, it was the best thing he could have done. I took a quarter and taped it to the wall across from my desk. Every minute of every day that I sat at that desk, I saw the quarter. It taught me a valuable lesson. I needed to stay hyper-focused. I needed to look at the metrics, the GPS of the business, and make those course corrections as needed.

I did not take any time off during most of that year. I took zero pay, putting those dollars back into the business and making sure we hit our bank covenants. Was it a humbling wake-up call for me? Yes, but it put me back on the right path and back to focusing and leveraging all the items we have laid out in this book. As you chart your path, remember that if you ignore the warning signs, you do so at your own peril. But if you stay on course and use the processes and techniques laid out in this book, you will stay hyper-focused, and your business will move in the right direction.

We turned the tide after that in-your-face wake-up call. We moved forward with the items in this book and supercharged them. We recommitted ourselves to not only live out the three C's but improve upon them. We went from one of the lowest points in the business during which we missed our bank covenants to creating a company that was truly special in all aspects.

As you chart your path, remember that if you ignore the warning signs, you do so at your own peril.

If you have reached this point in the book, I will assume you are highly motivated to create true enterprise value. Your goal is to move your organization from a good business to a great company and exit well.

It is my hope you have found some nuggets of encouragement and ideas in this book. This is a long-term process that cannot be done in a week or even in a few months. If you desire to take this journey, you need to start now. I can only guarantee you one thing: There will be bumps along the way. How you handle those bumps and keep your eye on the prize will determine your success. You will need to be hyper-focused.

You have built a great business, and it may have provided a wonderful living for your family. But are you on the path to exiting well? If you do this right, you may create not only wealth for yourself, but generational wealth as well.

I have been asked several times if I am happy that I sold the company. So many business owners watch their newly sold companies get absorbed into bigger companies with a loss of jobs and, in some cases, a physical move. Other business owners see their personal identity change after they sell. For many years, they were the president, the owner, the person in charge, and now they are (in their minds) nothing. Their identity is gone.

Am I happy I sold the company? The answer is a resounding yes! The most critical criteria for me in selling was to sell the company to the right organization. I wanted an organization that valued the team and was committed to making them successful. While the acquisition price was important, nothing was more important to me than the success of the team post-acquisition.

Some acquiring companies do not tell the whole truth during the acquisition process about what will happen to your company after the transaction. It is extremely painful to see a business owner filled with remorse because they sold their company to the wrong organization.

For me, it's been a few years since the sale. The number of team members who have left has been minimal. The best news is that the company continues to prosper. Teammates have been given bigger and better opportunities, much more than I could have ever provided. So, Carey and Danette, thank you for keeping your word on how you would incorporate my small business into your much larger one. In fact, several of my former teammates have been given more leadership responsibilities in the new organization. The sales team is involved in deals we would have never seen before. Like a proud parent watching his adult children succeed, I am simply proud of the entire team and excited to see their future.

Are you ready to take your business and build a great company? You are resilient, you have survived the ups and downs of the economic cycles, you have the courage. Take that next step in building your company. Your success tomorrow (and your ultimate exit) will depend upon what you do today. Chart your course, and take that first step toward a meaningful future.

I have spent several years testing this process with a few select clients. I needed to know if I could replicate the process with other companies. With all three of these clients, the process worked. One of the companies followed the process, and the owner exited a short while ago with an exceptional value. In fact, the private equity firm that purchased the company is replicating the process laid out in this book to all their companies. Imitation is the highest form of flattery. The other two companies have seen their top line and bottom line increase more than three to four times. Yes, that is four times improvement. The process works if you stick with it. While it can seem a little messy at times, if you have the discipline, you can do it.

As a small business owner, you are the backbone of the economy. You have taken risks, created a company, and created jobs. Most jobs in this country are from small businesses. Even though I am biased, you are among the true superheroes.

Use those superhero strengths, and create a company with a strong enterprise value. There are many ways to exit, and you will exit someday. The only choice is what it looks like.

NEXT STEPS

▶ What are your nonnegotiables in a possible sale?

▶ What are your exit goals for the business post-sale?

▶ Is a potential buyer aligned with those nonnegotiables and goals?

▶ Make sure you communicate the above clearly in the pre-acquisition meeting with potential buyers.

ACKNOWLEDGMENTS

DIDN'T REALIZE THAT writing a book that encapsulates how we created and maximized our enterprise value for our company would be so challenging. The biggest thank-you goes to my wife, who was my first editor, and my two girls, who continued to encourage me to finish this book. Thank you for your support, advice, and love.

I could not have accomplished this without my incredible teammates at the company. They were more than a little concerned when I bought the business over a decade ago, but they came to believe not only in me, but in themselves as we created something special. We were a family committed to each other and our common goals. Thank you for your perseverance and belief. Each of you is truly amazing.

I was also blessed to have a great professional team around me while running the business. I had an incredible group of bankers, lawyers, financial advisors, and CPAs available to help and guide me. You were a big part of this journey as well. Thank you.

I had a wonderful group of family and friends who may be surprised at some of the stories in this book. You helped me without knowing during so many of those difficult and challenging times of owning a business. Thank you never seems enough.

I also would like to thank my clients who test drove this process with me. I knew there was a little skepticism in the beginning, but you embraced the process, and the results speak for themselves. So, thank you, Mike and Chris, for letting me be part of your journey to create enterprise value for your companies.

A big thank-you to my friend Tom, who helped me through this process. I also want to thank the team of Streamline Books for helping make a dream come true. Your help in the writing, editing, and finally getting this book published was amazing. Thank you for your patience and guidance.

My goal is never to sell tens of thousands of books (it would be nice though). Instead, my goal is to help just one more small business to create true enterprise value and exit well. If this book makes one more business a little more successful, then the writing process was well worth it.

I wish you success in your journey to create enterprise value. It is at times lonely and sometimes scary to run your own business. Nobody understands the pressure until they sit in that seat. The failure rate is high when you run your own business; remember those sobering stats. But you always find a way to make payroll each time and manage cash flows along with meeting the expectations of your customers while hitting those bank covenants. Life is full of naysayers and doubters who will say you can never do it. I have personally encountered those individuals. But please continue to believe in yourself.

You have taken the risks of owning a business. Now is the time to create a great company. I wish you well in your journey as you prepare to exit well.

APPENDIX

Sample Metric Report

Weekly				Week Ending			
Prior	Current			W/E	W/E	W/E	W/E
Year	Budget	Area	Measurement	Date	Date	Date	Date
		Cash	Cash				
			Line of Credit Balance				
			AR - AP Difference				
			Total AR				
			Current				
			30 day				
			60 day				
			90 day				
			>120				
			Retainage				
			Accounts Payable				
		Tech Hours	Install Chargeable Hours				
			Service Chargeable Hours				
			V/H/ On Call				
			Non-Chargeable Hours				
			Total Hours				
			Utilization Rate				
		Installation	Backlog				
			Overtime hours				
			Write-offs				
		Sales	Bookings-Sales				
			Bookings-GM				
			80% Opportunities				
			Quotes Produced				
		Service	Service Backlog # jobs				
			Overtime hours				
			Write-offs				
		Invoicing	Total Gross Invoicing				
			Installation				
			Service				
			Central Station				
			Court Services				
			SaaS				
		Court Services	# of Units				
			Daily Revenue				
			Average per Unit				
		Central Station	Central Station				
			# of end-user accounts				
			# of dealer accounts				
			Overtime hours				
			Avg. Response time (seconds)				
			Burglar				
			Fire				
			Holdup				
			Medical				

ABOUT THE AUTHOR

David Nemmers, former president/CEO of Midstate Security Company, led the company to prominence as a top fifty security integrator with twelve years of consecutive growth. In 2019, he orchestrated the successful sale of the company to Allied Universal Technologies, the world's largest security firm. Nemmers is a former CPA with a Big Four accounting firm, Ernst and Young, and has worked in several different industries—from automotive to healthcare to furniture. With a background spanning executive roles at Turnstone, Gill Industries, and more, Nemmers is renowned for his expertise in culture development, team alignment, and leadership. A graduate of Aquinas College, he holds a bachelor's degree in finance/accounting. Active in his community, Nemmers serves on multiple boards and previously served as vice president of the Caledonia Community School Board. Residing in Michigan with his wife and family, Nemmers is also an avid runner with a passion for endurance races.

ENDNOTES

1 Biery, Mary Allen, and Sageworks Stats. "Study Shows Why Many Business Owners Can't Sell When They Want To." *Forbes*, February 5, 2017. https://www.forbes.com/sites/sageworks/2017/02/05/these-8-stats-show-why-many-business-owners-cant-sell-when-they-want-to.

2 Cohan, Todd Michael. "The Current Rise in Small Businesses Being Sold Over The Next 10-15 Years." *Score*, December 20, 2022. https://www.score.org/princeton/resource/blog-post/current-rise-small-businesses-being-sold-over-next-10-15-years.

3 Sinek, Simon. *Start With Why: How Great Leaders Inspire Everyone To Take Action.* New York: Penguin Group, 2009, page 39.

4 Kane, I.M. "Milton Friedman Defends Capitalism and KOs Phil Donahue's Feel-Good Socialism." *The Millstone Diaries,* March 8, 2019. https://imkane.wordpress.com/2019/03/08/milton-friedman-defends-capitalism-and-kos-phil-donahues-feel-good-socialism/.

5 Deane, Michael T. "Top 6 Reasons New Businesses Fail." *Investopedia,* updated April 1, 2024. https://www.investopedia.com/financial-edge/1010/top-6-reasons-new-businesses-fail.aspx.

6 Commerce Institute. "How Many New Businesses Are Started Each Year? New Data Reveals the Answer." Accessed April 15, 2024. https://www.commerceinstitute.com/new-businesses-started-every-year/.

7 Maxwell, John C. *The 21 Irrefutable Laws of Leadership, Follow Them and People Will Follow You.* Nashville, Tennessee: Thomas Nelson, 2007, page 7.

8 Rick, Torben. "How and Why Organizational Culture Eats Strategy for Breakfast, Lunch and Dinner." *SupplyChain247,* February 27, 2020. https://www.supplychain247.com/article/organizational_culture_eats_strategy_for_breakfast_lunch_and_dinner